IN SEARCH OF THE FLYING DUTCHMAN

He went looking for a needle in the jungle
haystack and found himself

Peter Gamgee

In Search of The Flying Dutchman

Copyright © Peter Gamgee, 2021
First published 2021

ISBN: 978-0-6450222-2-3 Paperback
ISBN: 978-0-6450222-3-0 E-Book

All rights reserved. Without limiting the rights under copyright reserved above, no part of this publication may be reproduced, stored in or introduced into a database and retrieval system or transmitted in any form or by any means (electronic, mechanical, photocopying, recording or otherwise) without the prior written permission of both the owner of copyright and the above publisher.

Original illustrations/ Photographs by **Peter Gamgee**

PROLOGUE

I am sure there are many who questioned my sanity, but wished me luck in any case.

I questioned my own sanity in taking on this venture. What's more, along the way, I questioned myself many times, and nearly every day.

Who in their right mind would set out alone in search of a 1942 relic into some of the remotest jungle mountains on earth? Into lands that even the local people do not go. In one of the most corrupt nations of the world. In the wettest season of the year. Over tracks tougher than Kokoda.

Put like that it seems like insanity. Or stupidity prevailed. But there was a motivating reason behind the adventure, which was closer to misadventure at many stages.

The relic was the wreckage of a plane that crashed during the war in 1942. A crash site that was last visited (two decades before) in 1986. Located on top of the Owen Stanley Range in Papua New Guinea. Near Ghost Mountain. The not-so-obvious reason for going there was a compelling desire to help people living in remote communities along The Ghost Mountain Trail to get better health and education services.

During this fourteen day ultra-trekathon I was pushed to the limits both physically and emotionally.

This is a short story of the highs and lows I experienced. Each day a story of its own. A solo adventure in that I was the only *taubada* or *white man*. But I was not alone as there were many local people with me who invariably helped me along the way. In return I was able to help them.

This was my last *boys' own* adventure. The demands of which were a brutal reminder that I was past my prime. And of what it takes to attempt *Kokoda on steroids*.

Temperatures ranged from five to thirty-six degrees centigrade. The sun was extreme at times. There was torrential rain at other times. Inclines were greater than fifty degrees in places. Kilometres of tracks were cut through dense jungle by hand.

Adding to these well known Papua New Guinea environmental conditions, there was sickness, leeches, falls, lack of food, infection and over-exertion. All wore me down physically so that at times I schemed of calling a rescue helicopter.

Even more than the physical demands, on the return journey I was worn down emotionally. I was asked by the local people to help some chronically ill relatives in remote villages. However resources at my disposal were limited. These are people surviving with illnesses and injuries that would be incomprehensible back in Australia. I did what I could to the best of my ability, knowledge and training in wilderness first aid. There was no choice but to leave a lot in the hands of the gods.

To leave each patient, to walk away from a village with these individuals on my mind, was difficult. I felt inadequate leaving people who were in dire circumstances. And with no possibility of knowing the outcomes.

Yet on returning home to Australia I remember the beauty of the lands around the *Ghost Mountain Trail*. Mostly I cannot forget the strength, consideration, kindness, courage and endurance of the people I met. People who live with a desperate need for the most basic services. For them dying at any age is just their way of life. Few live to be *old* as we know it.

Contents

Prologue v

Chapter 1: Why a Flying Dutchman? 1

Chapter 2: The adventure is almost abandoned before it starts 7

Chapter 3: First day out and the expedition is nearly cancelled 11

Chapter 4: More than a marathon to Lora and facing turnback 21

Chapter 5: Mission aborted … 25

Chapter 6: A massive weight is lifted off my shoulders
but I struggle to reach Laronu 31

Chapter 7 Strength returns but confidence in finding the wreck, dives 39

Chapter 8: The search party starts out from Laronu 43

Chapter 9: We halt well short of our plan and hypothermia sets in 47

Chapter 10: The new lands prove difficult to access 55

Chapter 11: Anticipation, excitement and disappointment 61

Chapter 12: We are blessed with fine weather and a speedy return to base 67

Chapter 13: It is amazing what a day of quiet reflection brings 71

Chapter 14: Day one of the walkout — kindness and horror 79

Chapter 15: My conviction is reinforced 89

Chapter 16: Unlucky for some and just plain hard work for others 95

Chapter 17: A not-so-simple trip to Port Moresby 103

Epilogue 107

Acknowledgements 109

Chapter 1

WHY A FLYING DUTCHMAN?

A NZAC Day. 25 April 2006 at Isuava on the Kokoda Trail. I was with a small group at the Battle of Isuava memorial. Our group had just walked the length of the Trail from the south. After lugging gear through exceptionally wet and muddy conditions, we were pretty smelly. Regardless we shared the ANZAC Day ceremony with other trekkers, including Kevin Rudd and Joe Hockey, a couple of noteworthy Australian politicians.

During that ceremony those who lost their lives were foremost in my thoughts. How they contributed to create the course of history, especially for Australia.

I observed the beauty of the land in the background, as the sun rose over the Yoda Valley. The morning mist highlighted with gold and purple-hued fringes, against the dark jungle green.

I thought about the local people, our carriers. And those locals of the recent past who had helped other foreigners. And about their ancestors who had survived and looked after this land for over 50,000 years.

I felt there was more to learn. And more to be done.

I would walk Kokoda twelve more times. Ten of those as a trek leader. With friends I also walked where few foreigners had ventured on parallel paths to Kokoda across the

Owen Stanley Range, those paths used by the Kiaps, the local Patrol Officers, on pre-independence patrols.

The Kiaps were the arms and legs of PNG colonial administration. They would travel to all the remote villages on a regular basis. Census taker, adjudicator, explorer, administrator, financial officer and all round tough and caring guys.

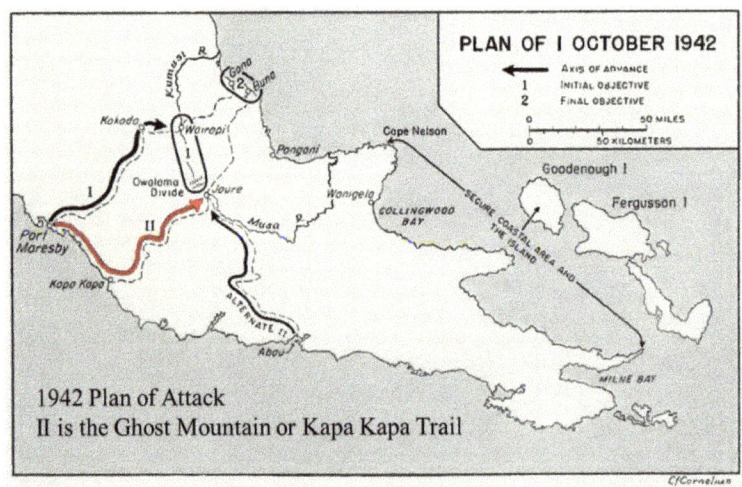

1942 Plan of Attack
II is the Ghost Mountain or Kapa Kapa Trail

One of those paths was *The Ghost Mountain* or the misnamed *Kapa Kapa* Trail running from Gaba Gaba on the south coast to Buna on the north coast. This track and its United States war history was first brought to light in 2006 by James Campbell's novel, *Ghost Mountain Boys*.

When walking the Ghost Mountain Trail in 2009 the needs of the communities in the vicinity were obvious, as was the potential for a sustainable industry. To investigate further, I returned in 2011 with my son Jake for a month in the jungle along this trail.

On that journey we stopped at all the villages. We sat, ate and talked in kitchens and guest huts.

We survived mostly on local food, including one meal of boiled green bananas!

We camped several nights in the mountains where there were no villages.

We made many friends and learnt a lot about the culture and customs. And also about the desperate need of people for simple services. Many services which had been provided prior to independence, but were no longer available due to the subsequent collapse of effective government administration.

We photographed and mapped the whole Ghost Mountain Trail. Hoping to raise interest and promote this trail as an absolutely possible trek, I released the book *The Kapa Kapa,* in 2013.

Since then there have been only four groups prepared to take on the adventure. The Trail was dubbed *Kokoda on steroids* by Lee Ticehurst, the expatriate Australian leader for James Campbell's 2006 expedition. The present walking part of the trail is about 225km with total ascent and descent equivalent to walking up and down Mt Everest from sea level.

In 2018 I had the pleasure of walking the trail with James Campbell, his daughter Rachel and other trekkers from Australia and the United States. Since then James and I continued to search for ways to help these communities. Rachel started by crowd funding for medical kits and school books.

We came up with the idea of fundraising treks in conjunction with *PNG Tribal* — a US based charity for PNG. There were several important considerations. That these treks would need to be of shorter duration than the three weeks it takes to complete the full trail. That they would be less demanding physically. And that the treks would be of interest to a wider group of people.

So the idea was born to trek into known US historical sites such as plane wrecks. The plan was to run two short treks, the first on the south side of the Owen Stanley Range, and second on the north side.

I knew of two WW2 World War Two plane wrecks that might create interest, which would suit fly-in, fly-out access and involve some significant trekking along Ghost Mountain Trail.

The wreck on the northern side was that of a C47-DL. *The Broadway Limited* otherwise known as *Quinn's Plane* had reportedly crashed into the side of Mt Lamington. This plane was dropping supplies to the Red Arrows 126th Infantry Regiment who had walked to Natanga from Gaba Gaba in the south. The Officer Commanding the 126th Infantry Regiment, Colonel Quinn had hitched a ride in one of the planes to supervise the food drop, thus ensuring his troops were re-supplied.

The parachute of one of the drops became entangled in the tail of the aircraft, causing the crash. All occupants died and their remains were recovered from the site. The crash site is just outside the village of Natanga. I have visited three times.

On the south side of the range was a wreck I knew about, but had never visited. It was that of another C47-DL *The Flying Dutchman,* which had crashed on the side of Ghost Mountain.

The plane was taking troops and supplies from the 126th Infantry Regiment to a forward airbase at Pongani on the north coast. They hit a sudden downdraft, clipped some tress and crashed head on into the side of the mountain. Of the twenty-three people on board, seventeen survived the crash. Of those seventeen, six lived to tell the story. But only after incredible survival journeys. One party of two made it out to the north, and the other party of four to the south.

When the alarm was raised about survivors, a search party retraced the steps of the party of two. Searchers got close, but failed to find the wreck, forced to turn back due to lack of supplies and difficult weather conditions in the high altitude.

Nearly two months after the crash local people found the wreck and a sole survivor. He was Captain Ted Baron a US Army Chaplain. However, he was so weak that he died whilst they tried to feed him bananas.

A diary was kept by the survivors at the crash site, written in charcoal on the cargo door. That door is now on permanent loan to the United States Air Force Museum.

I was confident I could take people to *Quinn's Plane* wreck and follow existing trails which I had already walked and mapped.

The Flying Dutchman was another story. Local people and landowners assured me they could take me to the crash site. I had some limited information as to its location from my own research. I knew it would involve cutting new trails and creating new campsites in mountainous area. There was too much risk taking a group of novice trekkers into such unknown territory.

The solution was to go in search of *The Flying Dutchman* prior to leading others. Already there were ten keen trekkers wanting to undertake the adventure. The pressure was on me as expedition planner, guide and trek leader!

The adventure was set and I committed to go, little realizing the life changing events that would unfold.

Chapter 2

THE ADVENTURE IS ALMOST ABANDONED BEFORE IT STARTS

Some people just pack a bag and go and seem to let the gods, or good fortune drive them. I prefer a modicum of preparation. Such preparations as working out how long the venture might take, what are the chances of finding the wreck, how much training I will need, how to survive on minimal conventional food, what the local carriers will need when they go into the high country, how much local money (in cash) will cover expenses, and how to manage security.

I trained. I lifted my running up to thirty and forty kilometres per week. I worked out a few hours a week on the hills with my backpack loaded to twenty-five kilograms. I got many strange looks from the early walkers at Kondalilla Falls and Kureelpa Falls circuits in Blackall Range National Parks close to where I live. I thought I was in reasonable, though not top condition.

My contact who worked at the PNG Museum was to get me the co-ordinates of the plane wreckage. Records that had been created and kept in the museum by Bruce Hoy, the curator from 1978 to1988.

I obtained information from the Pacific Wrecks web site. These included articles written by Senior Sergeant Holleman, one of the survivors, and other press articles and sketchy photographs.

A week before I was due to depart I had no co-ordinates to even get me close to the crash site. The records at the PNG Museum were *lost* or *in storage* since moving premises some ten years previously. Bruce's records were not to be found.

My thoughts were gloomy. How was I going to find the proverbial *needle in a haystack* with no co-ordinates for GPS? I felt this would be a disaster. A ground search over large areas of jungle, for a wreck that has been hidden by eighty years of jungle growth is impossible.

Should I just rely on the locals knowing where the wreck is?

To my sense this was not good planning, nor comfortable. I felt conflicted. Perhaps it was better to cancel the trip until I could get the information needed. Yet practically I felt unable to cancel this trip. I had to make this a success otherwise the planned June trip for which a few had already paid a deposit, would be cancelled and the whole exercise a waste of time. If necessary I would personally pay back any money people may have lost on cancelled airfares.

The worst outcome of all I felt was that the people in communities along the trial would miss out on improvements to health and education services.

More research was the immediate priority. There must have been some extra information somewhere. I studied every piece of research gathered to date. The stories from survivor Holleman, the records from Pacific Wrecks, some US quasi-military records.

Inconsistencies jumped out at me.

The paths taken by the survivors. The first group of four to leave the crash site were followed by a second group who left three days later. Yet the first group ended up on the northern side of the range, to the north-east. The second group ended up well to the south-west. How could that be?

Then there was the report from the rescue team sent from the north, stating they *turned right and went south-west towards Mt Obree, instead of left towards the crash site.* Based on the rough maps I had that made no sense.

Speaking of maps, it is impossible to get accurate published topographical maps of PNG. The best I was able to do was to extract them from Google Earth.

I started to piece together my limited maps and information into a coherent story.

It appears that the second group departing from the crash site initially followed the same direction as the first group. That direction was back towards Port Moresby, to the south-west. However, the first group had changed direction about a kilometre from the site to follow the streams, which curiously run to the north, even though they originate on the south side of the range.

The second group using the compass from the cockpit maintained a south-westerly direction and stuck mostly to the ridges.

This information together with the recollections of Holleman gave me the most likely area of the crash. At least within a matter of tens of square kilometres.

More research was needed.

I managed to find a RAAF compiled location map of crashed aircraft in PNG going back to World War Two.

Success, I thought. And they even have GPS positions.

I immediately looked for the two sites near Mount Obree, or Ghost Mountain. Surprisingly one crash site marked as a *B17* was a much greater distance from where it should have been, based on my research. In reality, how accurate was the RAAF location mapping?

The other crash site near Ghost Mountain, *The Flying Dutchman*, looked to be about right. The co-ordinates were approximate at best, rounded to the closest minute. But could be a long way off the actual position by as much as a couple of kilometres.

Almost by chance I then found digitised in the Australian Archives, selected records from *Kiaps,* the local Patrol Officers. I traced the year and name, Patrol Officer J Absalom, to the digitised version of a report made when he was sent to check two wrecks in 1961.

My luck was in. There was a report by J Absalom of his trek to *The Flying Dutchman* site! The report provides some description of his journey and a little detail of the terrain.

At last I was more confident. The Patrol Officer's report from 1961 correlated with RAAF location mapping, although approximate, and with the survivor account by Holleman. These diverse pieces of evidence more accurately positioned *The Flying Dutchman*, not on the side of Ghost Mountain, but on a slightly lower mountain range about one kilometre to the south.

The trip would happen after all. I believed with this new information and assurances from local people that they could take me to the wreck, on getting there, I would confirm the wreck as *The Flying Dutchman*. Confirmation based on location and inspection of the wreckage.

At least that's what I thought. Little did I know at that time what was to transpire.

Anyone who has worked in or tried to do business in PNG post-Independence (1975) will know that the phrase *it is not easy* is an understatement. Many continue to persevere for love of the country and sometimes for the sheer challenge. Perhaps I fall into that latter category.

Chapter 3

FIRST DAY OUT AND THE EXPEDITION IS NEARLY CANCELLED

After arriving in PNG I met up with my hosts. Bardey the ex-Chief's firstborn son, and two clan leaders, Didibu and Wairi. I was lucky to be met by such an important group of people, as they represent most of the community at Laronu at the foothills of the Owen Stanley Range. Also I have been informed, that Bardey's clan own the land where *The Flying Dutchman* is located.

Bardey and Didibu advised me that security was a problem on the way to the road-head where we were to start walking. And that I would need to hire a Public Motor Vehicle or PMV, a truck with a frame and wooden bench seats in the back. My plan had been to travel at low cost using the local PMV service for about K20 per head — hiring a truck would cost K700. I felt a little curious as to the reason but agreed to hire the PMV to make sure we would start early and get on the trail without any hassles.

Plans were set for me to be picked up at 7a.m. We would travel on the Magi Highway to be at The Junction drop-off point before midday. After a three hour walk from The Junction, we would overnight at the village of Odika. Over the following two days we would make our way to Laronu at the foothills of the Owen Stanley Range and our base camp for the expedition.

"Time" in PNG, especially in the country areas has a very different meaning to what most foreigners are accustomed. Very few in PNG wear a watch or are even concerned about the time of day or the time it takes to do something. There is night and day, dawn and dusk. My encapsulation of the difference is "you just keep going to you get where you want to be, there are no clocks in the jungle".

So it was not surprising that my early start turned into a long wait. The truck eventually picked me up about 9:30a.m. However I felt there was still a chance of reaching Odika by nightfall.

Then I was driven around several suburbs of Port Moresby to collect a few other people, men, women and children who climbed into the back with me. With little seating room left, I looked forward to getting on the road … quite a bit later than planned.

First we stopped at a store so the driver could get a new solar battery. Then we pulled up at the shops in an area called Six Mile. Here, the driver left us in the truck while he took some time to purchase stores for the vehicle owners' Trade Store or local village shop. These stores of bags of rice and sugar, boxes of canned food, biscuits and noodles, were loaded into the back around our feet and under the seats.

Our small party comprised three women, four children and fifteen men. Many of these travelling companions were taking the opportunity of a free PMV to return to their village, after spending Christmas holidays in Port Moresby.

I guessed it was just lucky coincidence that I needed that PMV for security!

I couldn't really blame them, nor did I have any ill will. If it helped them I felt that was great. And at the end of the day it was just costing a bit more than I had budgeted.

First day out and the expedition is nearly cancelled

The downside was that the early departure turned out to be a late one. Five hours behind schedule, it was well after midday before we set off from Port Moresby.

Along the Magi Highway we often slowed to a crawl to dodge or bounce through large potholed sections of road. After about three hours we arrived at the little township of Kwikila. This was a good spot for a break and was the men's final chance to purchase any last minute items at the markets.

I had no reason to get out of the PMV. Along with a few of the other passengers I sat waiting patiently for the purchases to be made. And for my travelling party to renew acquaintances with local people.

A policeman glancing at me, approached the PMV driver, sitting in the cab and exchanged words. I was the only *white* person in the PMV … and probably the only *white* person in the whole town.

I am used to being stared at but this was a little different.

The driver and policeman then called to Bardey to come back from the market. More words were exchanged in the local dialect. Bardey then walked back along the side of the PMV to where I was seated. He informed me that I was summoned to the Police Station.

Rather than walk the hundred metres we took the PMV. As the PMV bumped over the potholed road I began to feel curious and more than a little uneasy. We were escorted by three armed policemen in a Landcruiser.

After alighting from the PMV in bare dirt footpath that formed the Police Station parking area, I was accompanied by two policemen who politely showed me into one of the two rooms that formed the Station. About thirty other people piled in as well. The crowd was comprised of local people curious to see what was happening. We also had most of the men who had travelled in the truck with me.

Keeping the appearance of calm I entered through the first door wondering what was coming. Was I to be taken into the second room ... the lock up? And what was the reason?

There were four policemen in the room. A shouting match started amongst a couple of local people, two policemen and Bardey. It was all in the local dialect, which I could barely follow.

I clearly got the message though as I was the centre of attention.

If you had any recent experience in PNG you would know why I was wary about being in a Police Station. Was this a ruse to demand money? What excuse had I provided them to do that?

The initial *discussion* settled down. A policemen introduced himself and the others to me. He pulled out his big book of complaints. Then officiously, he read in partial English, the complaint against me.

He was interrupted before he finished and broke into local dialect. I could not understand fully the nature of the complaint.

Whatever it was, how could this be? I had been in Kwikila in the back of a truck for no more than ten minutes!

One local person was speaking animatedly. Accusations were not directed immediately to me but conveyed through Bardey.

An argument ensued. Voices were raised, there were scowling faces and arm waving with several people shouting all at once.

What I gathered was that the disturbance was to do with land ownership and rights of passage. Not understanding any more than this, I backed out of the direct conversation.

The heated discussion continued, mostly between Bardey and a local man. The policemen interjected from time to time.

To me it seemed that a second and elderly local person was being prevented from talking by the first local. There were also language difficulties for this elderly gentleman, apparently the real landowner, who seemed not to understand the argument either.

How would this end up? How would we extricate ourselves? I had always thought or considered that on lands nearer the wreck there might be landowner issues. It was a bit challenging to have them arise on the first day en route to the road-head. This was unexpected!

Half way through *discussions* the policemen decided there were too many in the room and proceeded to usher about fifteen out. Leaving the other fifteen!

In the background, one policeman started talking to me in broken English, to explain that it was a landowner issue. The landowners were there to sort it out. What he wasn't telling me was what they were after— a significant sum of money to go onto their land to find *The Flying Dutchman*. ? Is the wreck on their land or on Bardey's land?

I had already concluded it was more about money than passage or land ownership.

I spoke up at one point and let them know— *As there is an issue and the communities don't want me here, I will go home. This will save me money. But the communities will miss out.*

I wanted to convey that I was not about to give-in to extortion. Or to part with any money. The back and forth discussion continued for about thirty minutes more. Finally some part of my message seemed to get through. The land ownership issue appeared to be successfully contested in Bardey's favour.

I then made an offer to those making the complaint, to *accompany us on the trip.* Suddenly scowls turned to smiles. There were handshakes and words of welcome. My companions and I were escorted out of the police station and cheered on our way.

I subsequently found out that the police and the two complainants had been waiting all day for a *white man* who would be coming through town. They had heard a story that we were taking a trekking group across their land to the wreck. And the landowners were definitely there for money.

When they found out we were not a group of trekkers and that we were not going anywhere near their land, their case dissolved.

The whole incident took a couple of hours.

So much for the early start, which became a late start, which meant that by now it was late afternoon!

We climbed back into the PMV and were joined by a few other locals hitching a lift, who squeezed onto the seats.

Twenty minutes further along the highway the PMV turned onto a dusty dirt road. The road was really an unkept track across semi open savannah. It was bordered on both side by burnt out scrub. The road took us through the village of Boregaina. After passing through that village the road deteriorated significantly. The truck dodged and weaved its way along a precipitous ridge-line to the start of our trail.

The *Junction* or *road*-head as it was called, was nothing more than a slightly wider section of track with just enough space for drivers to make a many-point turn around. Off to the side was a narrow walking path heading north into the mountains. This was where sixteen of us – men, women and children, loaded up with packs and started walking.

By now the sun was going down … there was not much chance we would be walking another three hours to Odika!

Regardless, from the ridge top we plunged down a forty degree incline on the equivalent of a goat track. Although nearly dusk it was still about thirty five degrees and ninety-five percent humidity. In the fading light I sweated and scrambled down a kilometre of the narrow path through open grass patches and thick undergrowth. For an hour or so, I focussed on keeping upright, and on the head and shoulders in front of me.

When we reached the bottom it was dark. One of our team found a hut and a friendly local landowner who was also a village councillor. He would let us stay on the veranda of his store house.

Food was the priority. In Port Moresby I had proposed to buy food for the men (thinking a maximum of five) travelling with us to Laronu. Bardey assured me, *this will not be necessary. The men prefer and will get local food.*

That night there was no local food forthcoming from our host. After a conversation with the group they needed me to purchase a meal for thirteen men! Thank goodness two of the men with their families had brought their own food.

Nick and Breibio went off to the Trade Store or local village shop to get rice, sugar and tinned mackerel. They came back with rice, sugar and noodles. No mackerel to be had.

The afternoon's walk, although mostly downhill, had been exceedingly hot and humid. I had lost a lot of sweat by the time we had reached the river. My energy was a little sapped from the exertion. I also realized that somewhere between Port Moresby, the Kwikila Police Station and getting on the trail I had forgotten to eat any lunch. I was hungry.

With access only to a small fire to boil water I ate what was readily available…a 250gm pack of noodles and three *hard tack* PNG "Bigpella Man" biscuits. This proved to be a totally inadequate meal for the day ahead, as I was to find out!

Bardey's brother-in-law Nick, had prior carrier experience and had been a carrier on my last trip along the Ghost Mountain Trail. He adopted me or vice versa, as travelling companion and carried my extra gear. Nick was always looking out for me and assisted on many occasions.

That night Nick put up a tent for me. It was a good idea to prevent mosquitoes biting. Except that the temperature was still well over thirty degrees C. and the tent was so poorly ventilated it was like being in a sauna!

At the risk of exposure to malaria-carrying mosquitoes I slept on the veranda of the hut. I could only hope that DEET insect repellent on my exposed skin and the *Malarone* anti-malarial drug I was taking, would be enough.

It was a calculated risk because I have had malaria three times, and the cycles of fever, sweats and chills, tiredness, nausea and headaches are not nice! After this day and in this situation a good night's sleep seemed more important.

Other safety preparations for the trip included a SPOT Tracker. A personal GPS device that uses satellite communications to show exact location, and sends pre-set messages, such as *Travelling OK at this point, Camping here tonight*. The SPOT device also has emergency buttons to trigger specific messages for assistance or as a last resort, triggers international SOS and sends out my position. I also had a Satellite phone.

When we had eaten and before sleep, I went to connect with the outside world. First to trigger my pre-set messages and then to contact my wife Meryl by sat-phone.

To my dismay the SPOT Tracker failed to pick up a satellite. Despite repeated attempts, no messages were to be sent that way.

I was annoyed but not too concerned because I had the backup of a satellite phone. This is more expensive and a nuisance as the SPOT Tracker is a more reliable method of sending location information than relaying it verbally via sat-phone.

I removed the satellite phone from its protective waterproof container, turned it on and got satellite reception immediately, thrilled to get the network so easily.

I put in the call to Meryl but as soon as I did the phone disconnected from the network! I tried again several times.

The same thing happened. Strange, I thought as I had not experienced this before with the sat-phone.

I was out of communication. An hour on the trail and unable to let people know how I was, my progress, nor to call for help if needed. Without either of these essential devices, the SPOT Tracker or the satellite phone, how wise was it to continue into more remoteness?

I considered options. Would I have to call the trip off and return to Port Moresby until I could get the communications working? I knew if I did there would not be enough time to return to complete the trip.

I went to bed joining the others on the veranda floor wondering what tomorrow would bring. We would trek along trails unfamiliar to me for the first half of the day. We would move further from villages and towns, with no form of outward communication. It was possible that the problems with the SPOT Tracker and satellite phone were temporary, relative to the topography in this location and they could right themselves the following day. And I thought that Meryl would not hit the panic button ... for a day or so.

Bardey assured me our destination tomorrow, the village of Lora, was *an easy day's walk*.

I had an open mind. Although I had doubts as well about an *"easy day's walk"*.

Little did I know ...

Chapter 4

MORE THAN A MARATHON TO LORA AND FACING TURNBACK

When you know you are going to have a big physical day, you will usually prepare by having a good balanced, nutritious meal the night before. I had eaten noodles and *dry tack* biscuits for dinner.

You usually prepare by having a good rest. I lay awake worrying about the communication problem, about mosquitoes and malaria, and what breakfast would be ... five *Weetbix* with powdered milk.

The sustenance you have during the day, and pacing your physical exertion are also vital. Especially when the trek involves four climbs over three hundred metres elevation, six or so varying depth rocky river crossings and over a distance that locals consider as *a good day's walk*.

When I started out I wasn't too worried about my food intake. I knew those who survived *The Flying Dutchman* crash had trekked out of the jungle surviving on little or no food for more than two weeks. I was in better condition and had at least some minimal fat reserves. It should be OK, I thought.

There would be cell phone reception at a spot on the route to Lora, according to my travelling companions.

This gave me hope that I would be in touch with Meryl, who would then contact the Satellite phone service provider to check the service issue.

With a positive outlook for the day we headed off around 5:30a.m as the sun crept into the village.

The temperature would soon rise into the mid thirty degrees Centigrade. I was sweating heavily by 6a.m. and the sweating did not stop! We trekked up hills and down ridges until we came to the supposed spot for cell phone reception … there was none.

We walked until I was *running on empty* and then continued for another four hours. The last two hours, rain poured. We had been trekking strenuously for ten hours by 5p.m. when we got to the village.

I was saturated, exhausted, and feeling sick. As I staggered into Lora, I had lost hope for the whole venture. My thoughts during today were the gloomiest I have had for a long time. Not since my wife had a scare with possible cancer can I recall being so concerned about the immediate future. The inability to speak to Meryl had got me down.

The lack of communications played on my mind and I was trying to work out how I would overcome this problem. I thought I could buy time by sending a *runner* with a message and Kina back to Kwikila Police Station, where they could contact Meryl.

I imagined carefully wording the note. But the risk was that someone would pocket the money and no call would be made. To overcome this, I would ask the runner to witness the call and to carry back a signed note from the policeman stating that the call had been made. I recalled John, the policeman who explained events in the police station.

I imagined that these plans could buy enough time to delay the tripping of an emergency plan by Meryl. Then I could at least get to Laronu, to point the team in the right direction for the search, before turning back for home.

There was plenty playing on my mind, and I was not in great physical shape after the lack of food and the walk to Lora. Whilst I was moderately fit from my pre-trip training preparations, it was nowhere near enough for a journey with an energy demand that was the equivalent of two marathons in one day.

I started strongly the next morning, keeping pace fairly well up the first hill and down to the river. A river of sweat ran off me as we started up the next ridge, my energy lagging.

In all my experience with more than twenty crossings of the Owen Stanley Range I have rarely used a walking pole for assistance. But I was so spent on this climb that I picked up a green piece of bamboo lying beside the track. And I used that bamboo stalk all the way to Laronu!

Half way up the next hill at a gully in which there was a trickle of a creek called Sahoru, I had slowed down significantly. I felt pretty much finished. While we stopped to fill up with water, the last water for three or more hours, torrential rain started.

The decision was easy. There was no choice but to go on for at least another four hours! Eating was a problem. Heat stress made me too sick in the stomach to hold down food. With a dry mouth and forcing myself to chew purely to be practical, I chewed on a muesli bar.

I needed to get both sugar and salt in my system so I mixed up a water bottle of *super-strength Staminade* electrolyte replacement and drank the lot in one go. I have put it down to the *Staminade* getting me through the next four hours. That section of the trail took us up over one mountain range and down another. Meanwhile rain bucketed down.

At Lora village I tried the satellite phone and the SPOT Tracker to no avail. Sending a runner back to Kwikila and cancelling the trip was looking like the next best option.

The villagers welcomed us and provided a hut to sleep in. I don't recall eating that night. I can only think that I must have tried to have a decent meal although I was feeling unwell. Sleep, better nutrition and improved energy tomorrow, was my plan.

Before sleeping we made plans for the next day to take the steep route to Tabu village. At one particular point on the ridge to Tabu there *will be cell phone coverage*, I was assured. I desperately hoped for the resolution of the issue with the satellite phone or communication.

Exhausted I fell asleep visualising of being on that ridge, making that call. I was aware at the time that I was being what many call *cautiously* optimistic. In truth I knew I was hopefully wishing for success, albeit knowing the reality of PNG where nothing is ever guaranteed until it is done!

Whatever way tomorrow turns out, will dictate whether the trip is to be abandoned or not.

Chapter 5

MISSION ABORTED ...

I had a reasonable sleep. As reasonable as you can get on hard floors made from split bamboo poles. I woke many times during the night and my regular pattern of hard floor sleeping prevailed. Thirty minutes on my back, thirty minutes on my left side, thirty minutes on my right ... then start over again.

With every turn I take care to move gently, conscious of sharing huts with others. The huts are on posts that are not braced. Any movement moves the whole hut. One disturbed or moving body is felt by everybody.

Over the years of trekking I am used to this way of sleeping. I observe that for some reason, whether it is the hard surface or the regular movement of my body, my muscles feel more supple in the morning than when I have slept in my comfortable bed at home.

That night there were strange and vivid dreams. A common side effect of *Malarone*. On this trip it was more noticeable for me than before. Perhaps it was worse because of my physical and mental state as I had colourful dreams with scenes and events beyond my imagination.

For breakfast, I *lashed out*, knowing it was to be another strenuous day. This time, *six Weetbix* with powdered milk and a handful of local peanuts. Baked beans or spaghetti may have been better. Or even local food of baked sweet potato and yam as the others ate. But my stomach was not up to that.

We left Lora about 7am in clear weather with the temperature climbing. We headed for the drop-down to the first deep river crossing. This was followed by the first, longest and steepest climb of the day.

Our total ascent for the day was to be about one thousand five hundred metres involving two major climbs and two significant descents. Our destination, Tabu village at an elevation of around one thousand metres, is well known to me. I referred to the altimeter on my watch to judge where we were, more than I used time or distance.

I was sweating before we left Lora village as the humidity was very high from the previous night's rain and the sun was starting to shine directly into the village. A short way up the first climb and my clothes were dripping with sweat. As if I had swum across a river fully clothed.

I suspected that my core temperature was high but I pushed on anyway, setting the pace for the group, regulating my effort until I was just at the point of breathing hard, rather than panting.

About half way up the first steep gruelling climb I began to run out of energy. The previous day's travels exertions, a restless night and inadequate nutrition contributed to more of a loss of strength than I realised. I was debilitated or weak. Had I picked up a stomach bug? My stomach churned and cramped. It was difficult to eat anything and I resorted to a muesli bar.

The last part of that climb did me in. For the first time since I was gravely ill in Nepal in 1997 I was forced to hand over items from my backpack to Nick.

My pack to begin with was only around fifteen kilograms. This transfer of the satellite phone, food bag, first aid kit, rope reduced the weight to eight or ten kilograms.

At least I was able to carry that and did not give up my pack altogether.

My thoughts at the time were impacted by my physical condition. That's *it*, I berated myself. I can't handle this sort of trekking any more. It is time to give up on PNG. I will cancel the June fundraising treks. There will be no back-to-back Bulldog and Black Cat trek in April as planned. There is no way I could face a full trek along Ghost Mountain Trail as planned for October. I am past my prime. I am doing too much. I can't handle this trekking any more. It is time to retire from these adventures.

A little before midday we came across a solitary hut half way up the second climb. The men found a body sized piece of bark under the hut and I collapsed onto it.

Laid out on my back under the hut, I rested and considered how I was going to get through the rest of the day. How much would a helicopter cost to fly me out? If and when I got to Laronu.

Then I realised that to get a helicopter would need communications ... despair. All attempts at calls, had been unsuccessful. We had stopped for some time at the spot that *would have* cell phone coverage. Instead, there was absolutely no reception for my phone.

Such thoughts and semi-sleep were interrupted by a shout from the jungle and a return shout from the men in our party. A local man appeared and a discussion ensued. It turned out he had just found a pig in his trap close by.

Bardey negotiated to buy the pig for 100 Kina. The deal was sealed with a deposit from me of 20 Kina. The transaction completed, the pig was brought slung over the local man's shoulders. A fire was started and pig cooking commenced. All this seemed to happen in the space of ten minutes.

I knew the pig cooking would take two to three hours. So whilst the rest of our party remained to organise the cooking, Nick and I started out for Tabu, another two to three hours walk.

After a quick meal of *hard tack* biscuits, a muesli bar and drinking half a litre of *Staminade*, I felt well enough to climb. I recovered my items from Nick to reduce his pack size, in case he had to fit the pack cover when it rained.

The track *levelled out*. A loose term in PNG which means *not severely up and down*. We started to make good time and stepped up the pace arriving in Tabu before the rain, at around 2:30p.m.

The highlight in Tabu was an abundance of fruit — pineapples, bananas, cucumbers and watermelon. This was easy to consume but I ate a bit more than might be wise, for such a drastic change in diet.

That night I dined on local food. Taro, sweet potato, pumpkin and yam, mixed with a little tinned bully beef. Adding a side dish of well-cooked pork, the result of our transaction along the way!

I couldn't eat much but it definitely made the body feel better to be restocking, nourishing body and brain with essential carbohydrates, protein, minerals, vitamins and salts!

Even though my physical state was improving, the outlook for continuing the trip was dire.

In our post-dinner discussions I announced the facts to my travelling companions. *I am not able to complete the trip because there is no communication with Meryl and no backup communications.* I told my colleagues. *The best I can do is to continue to Laronu for one day and then return home. Do you have someone who could be a runner for my note to the police in Kwikila*, I asked.

So you need to talk to your wife? Bardey asked.

Yes. Unless I can talk to Meryl I will need to go back.

No problem, Bardey said. *There is phone reception just outside Tabu.*

You are kidding, I said. *Is reception guaranteed? Because the last two places where there was supposed to be reception, there was none.*

Asking for a guarantee on anything in PNG I knew to be somewhat of a joke. But this conversation gave me a sliver of hope. In the morning Nick was to take me to the spot where I *would get reception*.

My thirty-thirty-thirty sleep pattern that night was mixed with the hope that there would be reception, and calling off Plan B – a runner to Kwikila.

Chapter 6

A MASSIVE WEIGHT IS LIFTED OFF MY SHOULDERS BUT I STRUGGLE TO REACH LARONU

With low expectations and high hopes Nick and I headed off at 6:30am to the special spot outside Tabu. The description I had been given of the mobile phone reception location was a little vague and I had no idea whether it would be fifteen minutes or a couple of hours journey, so I carried a small pack, with a snack and a full water bottle.

My first pleasant surprise for the day was that the journey was around fifteen minutes.

Followed by a second pleasant surprise.

I had come prepared with two phones a Digicel SIM card, and an Australian SIM card that has international roaming. There was good BMobile coverage and my Australian phone and SIM card worked well so that I got through to Meryl. Feeling huge relief.

Meryl contacted Pivotel, the satellite phone service provider who checked the account and indicated there was no reason there should be a problem. They suggested I ring them directly if there was a problem. Meryl explained the impracticality of that when you are in the middle of the jungle.

The satellite phone was on because I had checked that it was not working before calling Meryl. Magically after Pivotel "checked the account" the satellite phone service came good.

It felt like my lucky day with three positive strikes before 7:30am. I was inspired by new hope and the expedition was back on track.

I hurried to Tabu to announce that we were continuing. I realised that a simple thing such as efficient communication had changed the mission and my mindset.

When I arrived back at the village breakfast was being cooked for the others in the party. Women appeared from huts all over the village with local food. Mostly yam, taro, sweet potato, corn, and cooked green shoots.

It was about 9am by the time we departed, loaded up with pineapple, watermelon, corn and cucumber to see us to Laronu.

My travelling companions were well fuelled with copious helpings of the local food in their stomachs. I am amazed how they are able to consume so much food in one helping. The volume eaten in one meal is equivalent to at least three meals for me.

That day's walking was supposed to be much easier than previous days. An initial steep downhill with about a four hundred metre drop in elevation, was followed by a ridge climb of about two hundred and fifty metres. Then a further drop of four hundred metres and a steady climb of three hundred and fifty metres elevation beside the Mimai River. A total distance of sixteen to seventeen kilometres.

Should be easy I thought, especially the last eight kilometres where the climb was gradual.

I felt good strong and we made good time. Along the way my mood improved, and I was thinking about preparations for the fund raising trips in June.

My physical challenges of the past two days were a harsh reminder of the terrain and climate to be endured by those people who I would take to see *The Flying Dutchman*.

It was up to me to make sure they were properly prepared. Instructions to them must reinforce, in the right way, fitness, agility and mental preparation for a tough trek. Reflecting on my experience over the first two days drove home the need for adequate training.

I am usually no slouch when it comes to tackling jungle trails. After many years walking with friends in PNG, the Kimberleys in Western Australia, tracks in Tasmania, and across England, I was given an undeserved reputation for being one of the strongest on the trails. The way I felt on the trail to Laronu I doubted if I could live up to that reputation.

If I struggled, then those less familiar with the environment and conditions would suffer more. Doing the *hard yards* in preparation was vital. I was deep in thought when we came to the village of Sari. This small village of about seven huts was perched on the top of the last steep descent to the Mimai River.

As is custom we politely greeted those in the village. The unusual event of having a *white man* in the village brought everybody who was not out in the gardens, into the village square. My travelling companions briefly shook hands with people they knew or loosely knew.

When Nick went to shake the hand of a young woman she put out her left hand and slid her right hand behind her back. The movement caught my attention as did the bright purple rag she had wrapped around her right hand. Did she have an injury? Did she need assistance? I asked Nick to enquire in the local dialect.

Yes, she had an injury and would like me to look at it.

As she sat on the steps to her hut she removed the rag from her hand to reveal the injury and at first sight of the gash across her fingers, the wounds were clearly in need of first aid.

Koko told the story that the day before she had been working (or fooling around) with her cousin-brother. As a consequence of accident or tom foolery, she had been slashed across three fingers with a machete.

The fingers were bound together with grass and congealed blood so that she could not separate them. Had this been in Australia or other developed parts of the world, such a wound would be treated at a hospital emergency department.

Koko must have lost quite a lot of blood and the hand was surely painful. But she was mostly smiling with the visitors and with the attention she was getting.

I organised for warm water to which I added salt. Most of the congealed blood soaked away and with Koko's assistance, the grass that was stuck in the wounds was removed. When she separated her fingers the full extent of the injuries was revealed.

The middle finger had a cut that would heal if it was kept clean. The next finger was cut about half way through to the bone and needed stitching. The little finger was cut to the bone. Muscle, nerves and probably tendon were severed on the fleshy pad at the top of the digit, with flesh protruding outside the skin. Koko moved the three fingers and joints to some degree. Luckily it didn't appear any bones had been broken.

In the next village of Dorobisoro, a two to three hour walk away, there was a first aid post which was usually manned by a trained para-professional medical officer. But I learned the medical officer was not at the village. He had run out of medicines to treat people and had walked to Port Moresby to resupply. He would then need to convince someone to fly the medicine in by charter helicopter.

Through a translator I gathered that Koko was considering going to Port Moresby and I recommended that she do that.

I cleaned the wounds. Then swabbed them with Betadine to prevent infection and bandaged them. I left spare Elastoplast bandages and again suggested she needed further help at Kwikila or Port Moresby.

Whether she would heed the advice I had no way of knowing. But I did find out on my return journey more than a week later.

After the hour or so attending to Koko, we were on our way, keen to get to Laronu.

The trail beside the Mimai River is one of the most picturesque of the whole Ghost Mountain Trail. It follows the river closely, crossing it in a couple of places. The terrain is gentle and there are three small villages to pass through before reaching the very last village of Laronu.

Normally I would enjoy the walk, but this was not the case on that afternoon.

About half way to Laronu I started to feel tired and nauseous. Was it too much pineapple? My knees were hurting and felt loose in their sockets. I was struggling to walk on that easy section of the trail. What I wanted to do was curl up in the shade of a hut veranda and sleep.

At the village of Abavana 2 I decided to give my body a short rest. There was only one man in the village at that time, the assistant pastor, who I engaged for a service of a different kind — to carry my pack for the next two hours into Laronu.

I considered the possible maladies I might be suffering. Had I caught a parasitic bug, such as giardia, or could it be salmonella bacteria or similar? There was the drastic change in diet that could have upset my stomach. It could be heat exhaustion or general exhaustion after three days of over exertion. The one common treatment I could think of for all these possibilities was the rest I needed once we reached Laronu.

Which we eventually reached about 5pm at the beginning of a torrential downpour. It had been an easy day's walk of only seven hours ... excluding stops.

The Ghost Mountain Guest House owned by my travelling companion Wairi and his son Eric never looked more inviting. The guest house is well constructed, for remote village standards, and nestles between the hillside garden, jungle and rushing waters of the Mimai River coming off the mountains to the north.

The setting is picturesque and tranquil. Even through my tiredness, nausea and burning desire for a decent wash after three days of hard slog, I appreciated the beauty. Tomorrow was a rest day and having a dry place to sleep for two nights without walking in between added to the appeal of the place.

As soon as Nick and I arrived food was brought for us. My stomach was starting to perform acrobatics by then and I could not eat much of the peanuts and cucumbers on offer.

Laronu was home to all my travelling companions. They were excited to be home and disappeared to join their families in the village leaving me alone to wash and settle in to the guest house. Clothes washing would wait till the morning.

Later most of my travelling companions from Port Moresby gathered in Eric's hut. There, sitting cross legged around the cooking fire in the middle of that hut, they recounted the stories of Port Moresby and the last three days ... whilst chewing and staining their teeth red with Betel nut.

My stomach was churning but I still needed sustenance to help my body recover. I dined that night on pasta with some tomato bolognaise sauce. This was not very exciting and was definitely short on protein but it provided the salt which my body was craving, and the carbohydrate for energy tomorrow.

At first I tried *Bully Beef* with the pasta but one taste and I felt sicker. These cans of ground meat produced in PNG, are greasy, very salty and to me tasted dirty. I had no trouble getting rid of whatever I didn't eat as my companions were happy to make sure nothing was wasted.

The next day would be for rest and organisation. Meetings would be held to plan the trek into the mountains where we would start the search. Those in the search party were to prepare by getting food from the gardens and sharpening their bush knives.

Community talks would explain why I was there and what was planned in the current search and for the future treks in June. Involving the community is important because we would hear details from the elders about the trail to the crash site and I looked forward to matching their descriptions with my research.

However any excitement that the search was starting was curbed by my temporary illness that night. Not only did my stomach tell me something was wrong, it revolted. I made many trips to the bamboo and leaf covered *long drop* located fifty metres from the guest house. My usual sleep pattern of segments of thirty minutes became interleaved with fifty metre dashes.

In a way I was fortunate. The brightest part was that the *long drop* was relatively sturdy and clean — the best since leaving Port Moresby. I would be washed out the next day and was again relieved it was a rest day.

Tomorrow I will find out more about *The Flying Dutchman* ... or so I thought!

Chapter 7

STRENGTH RETURNS BUT CONFIDENCE IN FINDING THE WRECK, DIVES

I slept in late and got out of bed at nearly 7am. I was exhausted from the night's upset stomach and trips to the *long drop,* although with help from *gastro stop,* the frequency of visits had abated.

After washing my dirty clothes and choosing the best place for drying in direct sun, I relaxed with GPS, a topographical map and my research papers. I poured over these, to form an idea where *The Flying Dutchman* may be found. And I wanted to remember as much as possible because I did not want to carry paperwork into the mountains as I thought to travel lightly.

Leaving the papers behind to save one kilogram in weight turned out to be a mistake.

The village meeting was a long and progressive one. Several leaders of the community had their say, asking questions, with responses given mostly by Bardey. I was not expected to be a large part of these discussions.

I was told the outcome was *everyone in the village is happy*. They supported our aims and would help with the search for *The Flying Dutchman*. It seemed that at least twenty or thirty men wanted to search for the plane. In the end about fifteen were selected, and agreed to spend the few days in the mountains.

I had been advised on every trip since 2009 that the locals could take me to the crashed plane, which they said fitted *The Flying Dutchman* story. I listened attentively to these stories as they were translated for my benefit.

Bardey's father took Bardey and his cousin-brother Kenix into the mountain when they were small boys, to show them the plane wreck. Bardey's father, the tribal chief, had hunted in the area and told the boys that his dogs had caught the scent of a *cus-cus* which was hiding in part of the plane. Bardey and Kenix never saw the plane because the temperature turned so cold they had to return home or risk perishing.

Another story was about a key landmark on the way to the wreck. This was a pile of rocks used for a *mumu,* a cooking method that uses heated rocks layered on the bottom and top of food wrapped in banana leaves. Once the *mumu* rocks were located, the plane would be along the edge of the adjacent ridge. Some of those present knew this *mumu* marker and were confident about finding the wreck.

It sounded strange to have a *mumu* at that altitude as banana trees do not grow at altitude. Perhaps they have another food wrap, I thought.

Then there was the story that people from Mt Brown area had walked through the land in 1943, discovered the wreck and taken rifles from the plane, hiding them in caves. The storyteller said he knew from descriptions in the story where to find the rifles and the plane.

I brought out my map and research information which gave a rough idea of where the wreck was located, according to the records I found. I was dismayed that not a single one of the local stories matched with the facts I had gathered. Could it be that the wreck of these local stories may have been that of a B17 that crashed on the southern side of Ghost Mountain? Because it did not fit the description of *The Flying Dutchman* crash to the south-east of the summit.

After questions from me and answers from the consensus of clan leaders, it was decided that the search area was to be on the side of Ghost Mountain where none of the current generation (up to 60 years old) had ever ventured ... not even for hunting.

We would be cutting new tracks through the jungle from the top of Ghost Mountain.

My hope that my research would supplement local knowledge was dashed. And my confidence in finding the crash site crashed. Locating the site would be based solely on an approximate GPS position and the information gleaned from multiple sources. I was disheartened. But perhaps not surprised by the lack of correlation between local oral history and my research.

I had suspected this might happen but had kept optimistic. I recalled in the report written by Patrol Officer John Absalom in 1961 when he visited the wreck, that he didn't walk from Laronu but from the Mt Brown side, engaging carriers from Saunom village. It is possible that elders in that village may have some recollection or knowledge of the location.

Was it worth proceeding? It now seemed our chance of finding the wreck was less than fifty percent. Was it now a waste of time and money to continue searching for the proverbial needle in a haystack? A site with eighty years of jungle growth on the side of a mountain with a potential search area of several square kilometres.

Despite the reduced chance of locating the wreck this trip, if I could get to the area with two to three days searching, we had a reasonable chance. I had to make the attempt at least. If I was to take an expedition in the coming June I would need to check out the trails, the access to water, the locations for camps and the emergency evacuation sites. That information was essential to taking a party of twenty people into the area. We would proceed.

The community did not need convincing. They were excited to go into their mountains and search for *The Flying Dutchman*. There were enough volunteers to organise two groups. The first to go with me to cut trails. The second group following a day later after Sunday church rituals were observed.

The *A Team* was a solid group. I was fortunate to have Didibu and Wairi the two most senior clan leaders, and Nick. There were six others — Numa, Kuname, Oerae, Odu, Simon (female) and Breibio. All but Breibio were regular hunters in the mountains, as tough as you can get when it comes to finding a way through the jungle, and having been raised on the hard work of subsistence farmers.

Chapter 8

THE SEARCH PARTY STARTS OUT FROM LARONU

Having regained my strength I was keen to get started. My idea of a good start is to move out before 7am, preferably 6am. Leaving early means you can cover plenty of distance before the hottest part of the day. It also gives a better chance of setting up camp before afternoon rain starts.

The objective for the day was to get to a new camp called Arakarea. This was at the junction of the Ghost Mountain Trail and the trail leading up the ridge line to Ghost Mountain. The camp had been established on a flattish area on that ridge. Only the previous year it was cleared to accommodate a scientific research group doing a biodiversity survey of the area. At the present time it was unusually occupied by an ornithologist, Brett from the Michigan museum.

After a while in PNG you learn to go with the flow. Bardey had scheduled an 8am departure. I nearly fell asleep again waiting for the group to assemble, for food to be brought by others in the village, packs organised and last minute discussions held. Just as well there was not a group of trekkers to organise as well. We eventually departed around 10am.

During the process of packing and assigning loads something happened that I was later to regret. I had prepared a small plastic bag of dried and canned food to supplement the local food of corn, yam and taro. I eat some of this food but to keep my strength and appetite I need to supplement with food my digestion is accustomed to. Most of this important food parcel was left for the second party to bring the following day. It will get to you OK, was the assurance.

Simon, the young woman, carried the majority of the local food in a giant *bilum* string bag slung over her back, supported by a band around her head. The weight of food was around twenty-five to thirty kilograms ... more than the men carried. The reason given for this was that the men needed to be free to chase game, in the event some appeared. Chasing through jungle after a pig is difficult when encumbered with a heavy pack.

I knew most of the day's trail from previous trips which meant there were few surprises for me. The most unsurprising day of the whole trip.

Within metres of the guest house the trail started a steep ascent of about fifty degrees. This initial climb was completed in an hour and then the trail became a steady climb, with plenty of rain ... and leeches. It was almost a pleasure walking constantly uphill.

We reached Camp Arakarea at an elevation of 1700 metres in less than four hours.

Once everyone was settled in camp I met Brett, the US ornithologist, and Bulisa Iova, an ornithologist from the PNG Museum, who is also from Laronu. They were collecting specimens of the birds in the mountainous areas in PNG. Brett had been doing this for close to twenty years with a trip to PNG every one or two years for about a month at a time. Brett had collected numerous species of birds, preserved them and taken them back to the US. The current trip was targeting understory dwellers.

Looking at some of the bird specimens Brett was preparing, they were beautiful and unusual. A lot of these birds once existed in Australia but over thousands of years as Australia dried the habitat was mostly lost. The mountain areas in PNG are a haven and preservation area for many species.

It was a noisy and happy camp that night as the crew in search of *The Flying Dutchman* shared stories with others from Laronu village who were supporting the birding venture.

I always ensure that the crew travelling with me have enough to eat. That night I was intrigued to see they had not attempted to cook any food and I enquired, what and when are you going to eat?

They would *eat in the morning*, to conserve food for going up the mountain. Later however, there were a few cobs of corn in the fire, steaming in their own wraps.

I went over plans for the next day with Didibu and Wairi. We would continue a further 1,300 metres in elevation to the top of Ghost Mountain. Here we would look for the ridge down along which we would cut a trail. By mid to late afternoon we would make camp on the edge of the grassland at about 2,600 metres elevation.

It sounded easy. I went to bed feeling good that we were on the way, that the day's trek had been relatively easy, and that we were going to be close to the search area tomorrow night. That would give us two whole days in the area, possibly two and a half.

With great and unfounded optimism I slept well despite the pounding rain on the tarp over my tent.

Chapter 9

WE HALT WELL SHORT OF OUR PLAN AND HYPOTHERMIA SETS IN

It rained nearly all night. My tarp and tent did not keep the rain out altogether, and condensation inside the tent meant most my gear was damp by morning. Rain at the altitude of that camp in January occurs more often than not, and as I crawled out of the tent, rain continued to drip from the trees. We will be wet a lot of the time today. Just get used to it.

We reviewed our goal for the day, which was to reach the grassland on the south-side of Ghost Mountain. The ridge we were following would bring us in from the West.

Looking at a map with no experience of the terrain you could easily underestimate the difficulty. On steep ready-made trails, a 1,300 metre climb followed by a 350 metre descent is considered a *solid but do-able* day, even in bad weather. It was going to be tougher than the map might indicate but I had no idea it would be a day when survival skills were to be tested.

The planned 7am departure occurred at 7.45am — not too bad given the usual delays. We walked steadily uphill on *reasonable* trails, meaning that we only occasionally had to cut vegetation or detour around fallen trees. And the gradient varied from gentle to very steep.

As we slowly climbed up the ridge the camp dogs that accompanied us were frequently disappearing into the jungle following animal trails and scents. They would completely disappear then suddenly re-appear in front of us again. It seemed the dogs thought this was a hunting trip and they were on the job.

When we were within about 300 metres of the top in elevation, the track was less *reasonable*, being overgrown in many places. The team got busy with bush knives and we continued at a significantly slower pace.

We eventually made the summit of Ghost Mountain around 1pm after a solid five hours of constant uphill walking. Breaking out into waist-high mountain scrub was a relief. It felt good to be out from under the damp gloominess of the jungle canopy … as well as to be near the top.

The exhilaration of summiting Ghost Mountain at 3,080 metres elevation had everyone in the party smiling and laughing. Despite the fact we had no view, and clouds were swirling over the top driven by a cool wind.

Next stage was to cut a new track through dense forest, jungle vegetation down a ridge running to the south. Didibu as team leader was keen to wait for a break in the weather so that he could see the ridge we would take to the grassland. He did not want to start out based on a compass bearing and my rough GPS co-ordinates.

I had to respect his judgement as he was the expert in this part of the world. I also knew that once we started it would be impossible to get a compass bearing to fix our position. The GPS positions I had from Google Earth maps, were based on my assumption of the likely path for the new track, and would be imprecise.

We halt well short of our plan and hypothermia sets in

The weather turned. It started to rain and the wind picked up. After sitting it out for half an hour Didibu decided to set up camp on top of Ghost Mountain but I was not convinced this was a good idea. The weather on top of the Owen Stanley Range can be severe. Temperatures below zero Centigrade occur even during a PNG summer. I was concerned there was no access to water, which was needed for cooking the staple rice.

The chances of cutting a new track to the grassland or of getting there before dark, were now slim. But I would have preferred to make some progress down and find an alternative camp site below the summit. I was not keen to remain exposed to the wind and weather on top of the range.

Our disparate views were influenced by the different thinking between our two cultures. I was keen to achieve the destination within a timeframe. To Didibu, and most of the local inhabitants of PNG, time is not an important concept. The destination will always be there. To that culture, time is relevant only as daylight and darkness. Doing something within a certain time does not make sense. You do things until they are done. You make sure you have time to eat and time to sleep. You must also have time to talk, to share stories and knowledge.

Didibu's call to camp on top of Ghost Mountain was not pressured at all by my trip's timeframe. We must wait until we can see the ridge we will go down, was his reasoning. If Didibu had been experienced in camping in cold places his decision may have been otherwise.

The rain although not torrential was being driven horizontally by steadily increasing wind. Meanwhile the men started to chop trees, collecting timber to make the frame for a *bivvy* — a tarpaulin over a ridge pole creating a rough A-frame shelter.

I stayed out of the way as these men know what they are doing. They are the local experts at setting up camp. So as they worked I had lunch, a large dry biscuit dipped into a jar of peanut butter. I sat to the side of the action, wrapped in a Bunnings green plastic poncho, while rain and wind steadily increased.

Simon did not participate in the camp building. Traditionally men build the camp. It was her job to carry the local food – and that she did, all the way up the ridge. Simon sat not too far from me huddled in her worn shawl. At lower altitudes it was not uncommon for the women and men to just accept that they would get wet. They are tough and being saturated is usually OK, but not when temperatures were plummeting below ten degrees. I managed to get her to cover up completely under one of the small tarpaulins we had brought.

One of the camp dogs had managed to curl up with Simon. The other three were not to be seen – I wondered where they had managed to get out of the rain. I thought they must know something we don't.

After an hour I looked around. There had been little progress making the camp. I saw an A-frame, in two places. The men had slung a tarp over a ridgepole and were huddled beneath, sheltering from the rain, and fighting the tarp blown by an almost gale-force wind. They looked wet through and wind-chilled. The rain got heavier. The wind swirled thick mist and cloud across the summit.

In frustration I wondered, why are they just sitting there? They are not getting the *bivvy* up. There is no fire. The camp isn't ready after all this time, when it usually takes half the time.

I got up. I had on a light down jacket underneath the poncho. The thin green plastic crackled wildly in the wind when I stood up. I looked around and found, a convenient length of green, centimetre thick vine to secure the poncho around my waist. Then I set to work … watched by everyone under the shelter, fighting to hold down the tarp.

First priority was for a secure rain shelter that would not blow away.

I headed towards the partial A-frame, just off the summit, slightly more protected. Roughly, using a machete to cut poles and some cord from my pack, I finished the frame in about twenty minutes. Then, out of the worst of the wind, in the next ten minutes managed to pull over a tarpaulin, tying it down to surrounding vegetation on one side, and pegged to the ground on the other. Every possible tie down point was needed to hold the tarp against the wind while crossing my fingers that the wind did not blow up stronger.

Next was to start a fire under that cover. I had come prepared — or so I thought. I searched my pack for a small box of fire starters and a lighter. The fire was critical now because I could see that Numa and Nick were close to hypothermia, they were shivering uncontrollably. Unfortunately, at the critical moment, sub-ten degrees at 3,080 metres, when we needed things to work, the cheap lighter I had bought as an afterthought from a street vendor, turned out to be a dud … it worked in Port Moresby.

I struggled to coax a flame from the lighter without success. After warming the lighter in my hands, eventually it gave an intermittent flame. Sufficient to light a few fire starters, producing a weak flame, enough to gain the men's interest. Two of them scooted over with handfuls of twigs and grass, to dry, and then to ignite. Fire instantly changed the team, who came to crowd under my tarp to build up the fire.

All the crew were not functioning as they would normally. They sat close around the fire. Two of them were still shaking uncontrollably. I directed them, take off your wet clothes. Put on dry things. Keep close to the fire. Whilst they were warming, I pulled another tarpaulin over the frame, to enlarge the area under cover.

Then I chopped down some reasonably convenient dead trees. While saturated, inside the wood was slightly drier.

I hauled the firewood under the *bivvy* to keep the fire going for most of the night.

Meanwhile the team sat around the fire. It was only later I realised they were confused — the classic symptom of hypothermia. They subsequently told me, they felt weak, all strength gone, could not think, and did not know what to do.

I continued working to put up another small tarpaulin with my little tent underneath. It would be cold and potentially sub-zero overnight and my best protection would be in the small tent. I positioned it at one end of the open A-frame *bivvy* to further reduce the wind whistling through the *bivvy*, and this worked to some degree.

The camp dogs were unsettled. One of them whining continually to everyone's dismay. The others were slinking closer to the fire, looking miserable. Even the dogs weren't happy to stay on Ghost Mountain.

After two hours around the fire there was a bit more chatter and even a little laughter. Simon had put corn, yams and bananas in the flames, and when cooked, everybody devoured these with gusto. I thought, eating is the best thing for them. It seemed to be a sign they were recovering. Also the uncontrollable shaking had stopped.

We all stayed close, huddled around the fire that night. The men and Simon told me they were now warm, thanks to every shred of dry clothing they had on. They appreciated the checked flannel shirts, padded jackets, light fleecy blankets, sleeping bags and sleeping mats brought from my hometown, donated by the Mapleton Mens' Shed.

The afternoon on Ghost Mountain had brought us closer. All the men let me know that they appreciated what I had done, making the shelter, finding firewood, and providing clothing and covers. They said they were amazed that this *taubada* (whiteman) could do these things when they themselves felt so weak. Normally it was they who would be helping the *taubada*.

We halt well short of our plan and hypothermia sets in

The chatter around the fire that night was much about what had happened that day and what everyone thought about what we might see tomorrow. With that in mind and by the firelight the one file we had brought was passed around and machetes and axes were sharpened to their users satisfaction.

The one blessing of the rain was that we caught the water spilling off the tarpaulins. Without that we would not have been able to boil rice and eat properly, because the closest ground water was too far away.

Our second group had arranged to meet us that night, bringing my food parcel. I looked forward to the protein. But they didn't catch up to us as planned, did they? I don't blame them given the conditions. Besides we would have struggled to shelter any more people in the one *bivvy*.

Instead I ate a couple of snack packs of macaroni cheese cooked with some of the precious water. Food never tasted better. Perhaps it was the warming effect rather than the artificial flavouring? My companions' meal was boiled rice topped with fresh water cress, noodles and five bush turkey eggs which they had found with the dogs' help earlier that day. I also ate some of that delicious topping.

I went to bed thinking over the day and the turnaround in events. Our progress up the mountain had been good. Until we reached the top I had been confident we would get to the destination of the grasslands on the other side. However, the exhilaration of *summiting* Ghost Mountain was soon forgotten in the bad weather and with the decision to set up camp.

We had now lost a day to search for *The Flying Dutchman*.

That night, before I got into my tent, I put on every dry item of clothing I had brought. Two shirts, a long sleeve shirt, shorts and track suit trousers under a slightly damp down jacket. Inside the sleeping bag I kept reasonably warm but the gear took on moisture during the night due to a combination of rain getting in the tent while it was erected, and internal condensation. The team in the *bivvy* may have been drier, but perhaps not warmer. Under the open tarp, they slept close to the fire and up close to one another and the camp dogs.

I fell asleep planning the next day. We would get off the mountain, down along the ridge line and be in the grassland by mid to late morning. Then we would set up camp before looking for *The Flying Dutchman*. We will at least get half a day of searching the target area, I estimated conservatively.

Little did I know ...

Chapter 10

THE NEW LANDS PROVE DIFFICULT TO ACCESS

I woke up well before the rest of my colleagues, eager to find the ridge down to the grasslands, and imagined searching that afternoon for signs of *The Flying Dutchman*. I was keen to get off the summit of Ghost Mountain to somewhere more sheltered from the bitterly cold weather. There might even be a small stream in the grasslands where I could wash.

It was a later start than I would have liked but PNG patience kicked in and I enjoyed the early morning views along the Owen Stanley Range. It wasn't perfect weather but it was clearer than the night before. The men were loath to move from the fire as we waited for sunrise and the weather to improve.

Didibu who is not familiar or comfortable with the use of a compass, wanted to be sure he could see the ridge we intended to go down before starting out. I felt frustrated that I could not direct the team as confidently as I would have with a decent topographical map, one with latitude and longitude marked. From that I could use the GPS to position us at any place on the map, and to keep on course.

Fortunately by 9am the sky had cleared enough so that from the top of Ghost Mountain we saw a hazy outline of the intended ridge which would take us to the grassland, although we could not see the grassland. None of the party, or any of the Laronu community, had been in the country we were to explore, even though these were their lands.

According to my rough topographical Google Map, the elevation drop into the grassland valley was about 350 metres. In normal circumstances, with an existing trail, this would take thirty minutes to an hour to complete. However where we went was not normal. The terrain was steep, the jungle vegetation was dense with plenty of large obstacles and we were making our own trail.

Cutting a trail in virgin jungle means a number of things. Beginning with finding the path of least resistance that is, the least number of trees, bushes, lawyer vine, ferns, bamboo vine, ant nests, jumbo bees, snakes, fallen trees, pandanus and nettles. Then cutting down enough to be able to pass through. At the same time avoiding severe drops of more than five metres (severe climbs are ok). Sticking to ridges except where it gets too hard. It also means keeping the momentum going by changing the front machete operators on an hourly basis. Making dual paths in some places to find the *least difficult* route.

To begin with the vegetation was thick and woody, high elevation heath and scrub. Tough going even with freshly honed bush knives.

We got into the moss forest about 100 metres elevation drop from the top. With less understory cover it was easier to see where we should be. There were however many more obstacles, such as fallen trees. In some cases the living trees grew so densely together that it was impossible for even one person to pass between them. We were careful where we put our feet as there was not much ground per se. Instead we walked on a dense leaf mulch layered on top of aerial tree roots. One step in the wrong place and your leg disappears up to the thigh.

At around 2,800 to 2,700 metres elevation we came across swaths of bamboo vine which hung in thick clumps down and across, from and to all other plants. This is the worst vegetation to cut through because it is fibrous and tough to slash, swaying away with the cutting action unless it is cut on exactly the right angle. Where possible each vine or a group of vines is held in one hand whilst slashing with the other. Through bamboo vine we progressed no more than a metre every five minutes. As you might imagine our trek down that ridge was slow so that six hours after leaving the summit of Ghost Mountain, we had not yet reached the grassland.

To avoid a precipice we veered off the side of the ridge, crossed a creek and gully, and climbed up the side of the adjacent ridge. By then it was 3pm and time to consider our options. How far were we from the grassland?

Could we find a site and make camp before the light drizzle that had lasted all day, increased to a downpour? Didibu decided to stop and make camp there on the ridge line. After fifteen minutes of exploration the advance party found a suitable flattish area.

I was keen to push on to the grassland. My rough plotting of our location showed this to be 100 metre drop in elevation. It can't be that hard, my first thought, immediately checked when recalling today's six hours. At that pace, it would be dark before we reach the grassland.

It took two hours, clearing trees, bamboo vine and scrub plants, to erect a camp. The camp *bivvy* was slung over the constructed wooden frame of about four by twelve metres. My companions insisted on building a wooden platform for my small tent that was erected under a separate little tarp.

Clearing jungle and setting up camp was what the men excelled at … when it was not cold. All vegetation was removed from twenty square-metres in a time that would make *greenies* cry and farmers sell their Caterpillar dozers. The activity distracted me from feeling downhearted about not reaching the grassland. Now we were two days behind my hopeful schedule and the search area for *The Flying Dutchman* was at least half a day away.

Just as the camp was ready, rain bucketed down and the temperature dropped at least ten degrees. Tonight everyone was happy. The men had shelter, plus two possums and a tree kangaroo caught during the day, again thanks to the assistance of the camp dogs. Simon had gutted the catch and put them in the flames to roast in their skins, before the last of the shelters were tied down. There was a protein feast that night.

However I felt conflicted when people caught, killed and ate the wildlife. My knowledge that many species are disappearing throughout the world caused me to think the wildlife should be preserved, even though I knew these people and many generations before them are hunters. Another example of our cultural difference. Local people have been catching and eating this bush food for tens of thousands of years surviving in the jungles. I observed that animals are caught with relative ease in these mountains, without an exhaustive search, indicating both skill and abundance.

Perhaps this country is not over-hunted, and the sparse human population is the main or only predator at the top of the food chain? Maybe there is a balance … provided that foreign trophy hunters are not brought in. This food was caught in lands not previously visited for hunting by the current generation. Would my quest for the *Flying Dutchman* unwittingly open a natural preservation area to sport hunters?

Despite these thoughts and armed with the knowledge that my strategy for future development included conservation, I consoled myself to enjoy a unique experience. Who else has an opportunity to sit under a *bivvy* around a fire in relatively unexplored jungle and be offered such delicacies to eat?

The second team that failed to reach us yesterday still hadn't caught up. I wonder, how will they know where we are? Have they even left Laronu? *It's the PNG way.* Time is not important and they will keep walking and looking until they come across our trail. They will follow the trail at whatever speed seems comfortable, and if they have left Laronu they will find us. Even if we are on our way back by then.

The missing team meant I was still without my food parcel. I knew I would not starve and ate what was available — mostly. I devoured two cobs of flame-roasted corn with gusto. Chewed through a fist-sized portion of roasted charred *German taro*. Topped all that off with a large metal bowl filled with noodles and baked beans … my protein for that day. The meal was scarcely adequate for hard trekking but I counted my blessings, at least I'm not doing the hard work of machete wielding.

My campions doing the hard work cutting through the jungle did have an advantage I did not. They had a constant supply of betel nut to keep them going.

The rest of my companions ate charred meat but I declined. I was offered a possum *drumstick* and tree kangaroo rib which I may have eaten if we had been closer to medical help or facilities. I had eaten bush meat in the past but they were so tough it took effort to bite off digestible pieces.

By torchlight later that night I calculated and plotted our position on the map. We were about 2,760 metres elevation. This ridge seemed to be better for a descent from the top of Ghost Mountain than the one we had started with. We were only a 60 to 100 metre drop in elevation to the grasslands … So close.

I re-calculated the days at my disposal and when to be back in Port Moresby for the flight home. I was disappointed to have only one day on the mountain to look for *The Flying*

Dutchman, and we hadn't even started looking yet. Could I delay my return home and my flight? Yes, I could but I wanted and needed to be home for Meryl and business. Best to keep to the planned schedule.

Wait and see what tomorrow brings.

Chapter 11

ANTICIPATION, EXCITEMENT AND DISAPPOINTMENT

The rain continued most of the night and we woke to a rather fresh morning with the rain water still dripping from the trees but this did not dampen the enthusiasm. Everyone was excited to get on with the search and we started out at 7.15am. I decided to call this site Camp Hope. We would return to the camp that night to save us establishing a new camp. Simon stayed in the camp alone with one of the camp dogs.

I was the only one to take a pack to hold the safety and navigation gear and my lunch. Travelling light and with renewed energy the trail down the ridge was cut quickly. By 8.30 we were at the edge of the grassland. After the gloom of the jungle over the past few days I emerged with relief into an open area lit by shards of weak sunlight.

I suspect some of the men had not believed there was a grassland here because they were not able to see it from the top of Ghost Mountain. Nor had any of them been in the area before. As we left the jungle behind and reached the open, they and the dogs ran off in different directions exploring the new place. Or looking for another meal-on-legs as that type of country supports ground-dwelling wallabies. The fact that we had reached grassland, and that it was where I said it would be, renewed their anticipation and eagerness to find *The Flying Dutchman*.

I checked position and bearings, pointed out the direction of the wreck and suggested we travel up the ridge to the search area. However, after a short discussion the consensus was to make a path beside the creek instead of my ridge suggestion. I acquiesced to their experience but in retrospect this lead us literally *up the creek*.

I followed behind, from time-to-time checking the GPS reference and direction to the approximate position of the wreck. We came to a gap in the range and the top of a ridge line. The terrain was what I expected had we been on track to the wreck location, according to the Google topographical map. We are here and ready to search ... so I thought.

But the location did not agree with the wreck-site GPS bearing, which I had recorded. I did not realise it at the time, but the creek we followed had veered off course and led us on the wrong ridge line. One that was not recognisable from the map.

For a while I was confused. Our position seemed to fit with map indications and the terrain on either side of our position. However the GPS indicated our destination was a further 360 metres to the south. I was unable to get a compass bearing from any feature such as Ghost Mountain, due to the dense vegetation, and there being no vantage point.

We started to search, but eventually I realised, this is wrong ... we are on the wrong ridge. My navigation had been inadequate. If only I'd been equipped with a contour map with latitude and longitude, and not been swayed by the *easy path up the creek*.

The vegetation was so dense it was impossible to see more than twenty metres. Difficult to see a wreck from any distance. The area around *The Flying Dutchman* had been cleared I thought around 1986 when Bruce Hoy took pictures of the wreck. I thought the keen eyes of my companions would observe this even seven decades later, as a difference in the vegetation, before sighting any wreckage. Needle in a haystack, was ringing in my mind.

Eventually we trusted the GPS and cut a path as direct as possible — definitely not straight — to the location I had entered in my handheld GPS. The position was to one I had obtained from the RAAF database on crashed aircraft in PNG.

We descended into a gully and then climbed a small range running in an east-west direction, to the south of Ghost Mountain. The straight line was over the top of a peak so we skirted to the east through a gap in the range. Finally we traversed the south-side of the range at about 2,700 metres, the same altitude as the gap, until we came to the GPS location. Everyone was becoming more excited the closer we were, with men and dogs searching up and down the sides of the severely steep terrain.

Nick shouted … he had found something. At incredible speed given the terrain all the men raced towards Nick. But it soon became clear it was a false alarm.

We continued the search for a few hundred metres up, down and to either side.

I sat down to survey the terrain and specific location. The altitude was about correct, corroborated by all the pieces of information I had obtained. The position relative to Port Moresby was also correct. We were on the south-side of this range. *The Flying Dutchman* had been flying north-east to Pongani. Logic was that it would have crashed into the south-side of the range.

What was not right to me was the steepness of our location because photographs of the wreck and descriptions from the survivors indicated the crash site was much less steep. Above and below the crash site had been steep, but the impact was in a *flattish* area and there was no flattish area where we were.

The GPS position from the RAAF database was approximate, at best, rounded to the nearest minute in latitude and longitude. The error of rounding would be up to 1.3 kilometres in any direction. Assuming the GPS position was correct in the first place the crash site could be up to 1.3 kilometres away ... in any direction.

Some in the team previously had seen me use the GPS to accurately show our location but they did not know that this was because I had previously mapped and entered those locations. Now they were having trouble understanding why the wreck was not at this GPS location.

After an hour of searching it was mid afternoon. Time to return to camp. I was disheartened. Realistically I did not think finding the plane would be easy. The GPS position was not precise but I had hoped that local people knew where the wreck was, and that the approximate GPS position would help to confirm it was *The Flying Dutchman*. More information was needed to find the proverbial needle in this haystack of dense tropical jungle. With reluctance we returned to camp and got in just before the rain started.

Whilst I do not understand the local dialect nor the quiet chatter as we settled back into camp, I sensed the disappointment. They wanted to be the ones to find the wreck site.

Alone in my tent as the rain pelted down I studied the maps and GPS positions, and re-traced our journey of that day. I saw how we had ended up on the wrong ridge to begin with. A mistake that cost us a couple of hours search time, which in the normal scheme of things in PNG is no time at all.

Before we left Laronu to trek up the mountain I had unpacked and left behind all items considered unnecessary, including the heavy folder of background research information on the crash site. Now I regretted leaving behind the paperwork with Patrol Officer John Absalom's 1961 report, SSGT Holleman's description of his journey from the crash site, and the description of the attempted rescue from the North, and the path they took.

From inside the tent I could hear that the men around the fire were more cheerful as the two possums caught that day on the way back to camp, were roasting.

At 5pm I heard the men respond to a call from the summit of Ghost Mountain. The second team, due to have reached us two days ago, was on its way. Two hours later four men and a woman plus two dogs arrived at the camp to join the others around the fire. This team started out two days after we left Laronu and were two days overdue because they took an alternate path up the mountain.

That night I enjoyed some of my own food – reconstituted lamb curry with rice and a can of spaghetti on the side.

Both teams sat around the fire discussing the day's events. Joe, a member of the new group gave his reasoning as to why we would never find the plane with a GPS device ... because that is not the traditional way, he claimed.

Joe had been one of the carriers with the group I was leading on The Ghost Mountain Trail in 2018. On that trip we had difficulty finding one section of trail, which is a story in itself. The section we were walking lead to an old village site of Rirembe, a 1942 camp for the US, 126th Infantry Regiment on their march across the Owen Stanley Range.

Yes, the locals from Laronu knew the route. I checked that before we departed from the main track.

Not long after we made this turn towards Rirembe the lead carriers started cutting a new track because they had lost the old one. I had walked the old trail before and had it in my handheld GPS so I directed them back to the correct trail and did this twice more before we found and kept on the old trail.

At Rirembe we had expected a fully prepared camp with new carriers waiting to take us along the northern section of the trail. But we got there to find no-one and no camp prepared. Adding to the challenge, it started pouring rain and the two carriers with the tarpaulins had disappeared whilst hunting. Those hunters had decided to bypass Rirembe and go direct to our destination for the next day.

Joe had misunderstood that it was by following the GPS map that the group had lost the trail.

This story was Joe's evidence that the GPS would *"bugger up"*, because it was not the traditional way. As a result, Joe would take his party along our trail tomorrow to search in accordance with stories he had heard, that people from the Mount Brown side had found the crash site, taken rifles and hidden those rifles in a cave.

I went to sleep that night thinking about today's disappointment. And how useless it was to search without enough information on the exact location of the crash site. I hoped Joe and his team, using the traditional ways, would be successful in searching tomorrow, as my team headed back to Laronu.

Given the difficult conditions and inability to find the plane wreck I had serious doubts about continuing with the fundraising trek. I would cancel the trips and close the book on supporting the communities along Ghost Mountain Trail. There was certainly no way to safely take a group of trekkers over the terrain where I had been.

Chapter 12

WE ARE BLESSED WITH FINE WEATHER AND A SPEEDY RETURN TO BASE

We woke to fine weather and broke camp by about 7.30am. I was keen to get back to Laronu the same day, retracing what had taken three days on the way up. We gained the summit of Ghost Mountain in under two hours, scrambling up the trail it had taken us over six hours to cut.

The weather was perfect on top. Such a contrast to the miserable night we had three nights previously. It was good to be warmed in the sun. We could see in all directions with scarcely a cloud to impede the view to the horizon. My focus immediately went to where we had searched for *The Flying Dutchman* the day before. I clearly saw the range we had been behind. And the ridge that deceived me initially.

I looked around at the terrain to the east and matched that with the map I was carrying. We were in the right place on the south-side of that range. Everything I recalled from the research seemed to correspond with what I saw, which made me eager to return to Laronu to re-examine the research material for further clues.

After soaking up the sunshine for nearly an hour we pushed on down the ridge towards Laronu at a jog. By midday we were back at Camp Arakarea. We had taken just four hours to complete what had taken two days on the way in. The significant difference was that we were going downhill instead of up and not cutting trails.

At Camp Arakarea I spent time talking to Brett, the ornithologist gathering museum specimens. Brett was pleasant and happy to chat telling me of studying birds in PNG for more than twenty years, most of the trips in remote locations under harsh conditions. Since our leaving the camp a few days ago, Brett assisted by a team of men from Laronu had erected 500 metres of bird netting to catch understory birds. As we talked, he was in the process of gutting and preserving a specimen caught that morning — a bird with colourful blue and white spots on its wings. There were ten to twenty cotton bags hanging from a long line under the tarp roof of Brett's work area, each bag containing a live bird to be preserved as a specimen.

As I snacked on hard tack biscuits and peanut butter before we continued, I couldn't help but wonder whether there is science behind the number of specimens being collected? I hoped they were not being over harvested.

My optimistic schedule set at the beginning of the day was to be back in Laronu before dark so I was surprised when, as one of the three men in the lead, I arrived at the guest house just after 2pm. On the last steep stretch as the track dropped the last 400 metres in elevation to Laronu my legs felt a little like jelly. We had virtually jogged all the way down the descent of 2,300 metres in under four hours and *jelly legs* combined with a wet track caused a couple of slips and falls.

An hour and a half later all of the team was back at base. I hadn't washed for five days and was desperate to plunge into the river but held off until I welcomed everyone into

We are blessed with fine weather and a speedy return to base

camp and thanked them for a great safe trip. Not used to being thanked, I saw that they appreciated it.

The Mimai River was a mere 50 metres from the guest-house. I stripped to my underwear and plunged into the cool water. After five days it was a real pleasure to be well and truly clean. I inspected numerous itchy insect and leech bites, checking for infection, and attended to scratches and grazes from the falls.

Around the kitchen fire that night most of the men from the search party recounted stories of the trip. They told where the trails were cut, the hunting, where water was obtained, and of course the comical events, shared with about twenty who had gathered to listen. Several times the story was told about the *taubada, white man* who put up camp on top of the mountain when everyone else was too cold and had no energy. I am now a local legend. No other *taubada, white man* had camped on top of Ghost Mountain or acted the way I had.

They talked excitedly about discovering the new land. There was much conversation about how and when they would go back up into the area with all the men and women from the village, to find *The Flying Dutchman*.

Dry, warm and comfortable in the guest house that night, thoughts turned to home. I had gone to the furthest part of my journey, it was natural that home was on my mind. I pondered the many things that would be waiting for me. After trips like this there would inevitably be projects that Meryl had for me at home, home maintenance or repairs to be done. I had business to attend in order to earn a living. There was a pending operation on my hand after which I would be out of commission for manual work for six weeks. And there would be physical training preparation for five further treks I was to do that year.

One thing I was desperate to do, was to gather more information about the crash site so that I could better direct the search.

I considered the wisdom and risk associated with taking trekkers where we had been. The terrain and trails are only suitable for prepared, and experienced trekkers, and even then the risk is high. I had been lucky not to sustain serious injury mainly because I am conscious of being careful ... as much as you can whilst travelling at the local's pace. If an accident happens there is little or no immediate support, and I wanted to avoid the need for search and rescue or *medivac*.

My thoughts were in conflict that night. Wanting to locate *The Flying Dutchman*, wanting to make sure the right thing was done for the local communities and wanting to reduce risk for trekkers. Then considering cancelling the forthcoming trek as I analysed whether or not I could run a viable trip.

Home is comfortable with many services people take for granted. There are no such services for the people along the Ghost Mountain Trail and in many other places in PNG.

The next day was a rest day to work through future plans before leaving Laronu. Once home I would access the resources to locate *The Flying Dutchman*.

Chapter 13

IT IS AMAZING WHAT A DAY OF QUIET REFLECTION BRINGS

A late start for me ... I didn't get up until 6.30am. First priority was to wash all my clothes in the river, to give them a chance to dry during the day on the washing line between two trees at the side of the guest house, or draped over vegetation by the river.

Wairi and his son, Eric who runs the Ghost Mountain Guest house, had erected a tarpaulin, with a rough hewn table and bench seat off to the side of the guest house. This was Wairi's idea and just for my use. Only one of many displays of consideration I was to experience on my return journey.

I spent two hours poring over all my research material. I plotted our track in detail, trying to fit the facts from Patrol Officer John Absalom's report, SSGT Holleman's description, a photo attributed to Bruce Hoy ex-curator of PNG Museum, and the terrain I had observed.

John Absalom reported *walking to the end of the tundra to wait for the carriers to return*. These were the carriers who had gone in search of *The Flying Dutchman* and returned with pieces from the wreck. I matched the *tundra* with the contour map and Google Earth imagery of a grassland at around 2,400 metres. Based on the description of how Absalom had arrived at the *tundra*, I determined that he had most likely walked to the eastern end.

I knew from many sources of information that the elevation of the crash site was 9,000 feet ... 2,743 metres on my contour map.

From the description given by SSGT Holleman, and the photo attributed to Bruce Hoy the plane had landed in a *flattish* area on the side of the mountain.

What had always bothered me was the description by the search party, which had set out to retrace the steps of the two survivors who ended up at Safia to the north-east. The searchers described getting close to the crash site and finding a pair of army leggings on top of a rock. From this point they, *went left and travelled south-west towards Mt Obree where they hoped to get a view of the crash site.*

The report also stated that had they gone *right* (to travel north-east) they would have come across the crash site. Eventually this search party turned back as they were not equipped for the cold, and had run out of supplies. However I could not match this information to the other descriptions, nor the likely route taken by those survivors whose steps the search party was retracing.

Prior to leaving for PNG I had mapped that route on Google Earth based on the evidence that the two survivors started out from the crash site to the south-west but then followed the creeks and rivers to end up on the Moni River, which flows in to the Musa River. I concluded that the search party descriptions were inaccurate and not worth considering now.

The balance of all the other information meant I was looking for a *flattish* area at 2,743 metres, somewhere above the eastern end of the grassland. I scoured the map area defined by the GPS rounding error, from our position during the search two days previously.

There is only one location that appears to meet all the criteria.

As I checked and re-checked and focussed on every detail of the map, I became more convinced that based on the research descriptions, I now knew the most likely position of the crash site. I was excited, regretful and annoyed. Oh, if only I had this information up on the mountain two days ago, I would have stayed longer.

I calculated that the crash site was most likely to be only 800 to 900 metres to the east of where we had been searching. With a permanent black marker I circled the position on the map.

Then I started thinking about the logistics if this was the crash site. The local people would search again to confirm it. Then I would need to work out how to get trekkers in and out safely. A group of trekkers could not follow the tracks I had been along. The climb up and over Ghost Mountain would also be difficult for some people, especially if it was their first experience trekking in those conditions.

I also needed to consider the carriers who would be supporting the expedition. The local people were not used to the cold. A couple of them had been fully trained as carriers on trails like Kokokda but in general they were not used to looking after trekkers' needs.

The trek must not be too taxing. It is vital to have adequate shelter and fallback options if there was bad weather, as well as emergency evacuation points should they be needed. I studied the maps again, for possible fixed camp sites where basic camp facilities could be pre-established. I came up with a plan based on two camps. The first site would be at Arakarea where we had stayed on our first night up the mountain. The second could be on the edge of the grassland on the other side of Ghost Mountain, *The Flying Dutchman Camp*.

This plan would require new trails to be cut to the west of the Ghost Mountain summit. The elevation along that trail would rise to about 2,850 metres and on a much easier gradient than going over the top of the mountain. This would come out at an altitude and location to make an easy traverse to the site that seemed to be the most likely crash position.

I was refreshed mentally that there was a way ahead. We had a good chance to find *The Flying Dutchman*, and I had a plan for the trail and logistics making the trek viable and within acceptable risk. I wanted to share these thoughts with Didibu, Bardey and Wairi to get their input and agreement but I had to wait until the discussion planned that night.

I was keen also to hear how the second search team had gone in *the traditional way*. They were not due back until late. Had *they* found the crash site?

I spent the rest of the day on practicalities. Drying my boots, my tent and the washing, in between light rain showers. I sorted my gear and food, gifting whatever I did not need to various Laronu people. Brian, my travelling companion as a school kid in 2009 and 2011, and then as a carrier in 2015, scored my tent.

During the day I had time to myself to reflect on the highs and lows of the journey. I recalled some of the events, the places we had been, chats around smokey fires at night, and all the experiences both good and bad. It seemed I had packed a year's worth of experience into less than two weeks. How was I going to be able to explain what I had been through to family, friends and people at home?

Physically, my days for such adventures are numbered. I could no longer keep up the pace or, perhaps deal with the risks associated with such expeditions. My aerobic capacity is not up to it, my skin is getting thinner and scratches more easily, my knees ached most of the time, and I didn't have the strength to carry a full pack over this terrain.

I looked around the village in its idyllic setting. I remembered the nights around the camp fire, making virgin trails to new lands and I knew I was going to miss this.

I was torn in different directions, knowing that there was more to do to make any changes sustainable for the communities. They need better services, especially health and education. There is more opportunity for them if they can get produce such as peanuts, yams and bananas to market. Conservation of their land and sustainable farming such as chicken and egg production to offset the reduced hunting, was another possibility.

I began to write out the story of my trip, sketching out the first few pages sitting at the bench under the tarpaulin that Wairi and Eric had put up for me.

Meanwhile in the main part of the village, there was a bit of activity. Bardey had convinced his relatives to kill a pig and celebrate the life of his two elderly aunts, his father's sisters. The reason was that he feared he may not see them again after he returned to Port Moresby with me.

A *mumu* was prepared. In the morning, one of the biggest village pigs was caught by the young boys. The struggling pig soon had its throat cut and was butchered bush-style by young men with very sharp bush knives. The pieces were well washed in the river by the men and the women then took pieces of the carcass to layer in a shallow pit over fire-heated rocks covered with banana leaves. Whole washed vegetables had been brought from the gardens and these were also layered around the meat and between banana leaves. More banana leaves and hot rocks made a lid over the ground oven and the food was left to bake for several hours.

I was sitting chatting with Wairi at the guest house, which is three bridges and a 100 metre walk from the main village area. Around 4.30pm I was surprised when what might be considered *Uber Eats* arrived for me ... without putting in an order. The meal was delivered by a couple of timid young women. The food was in a well used, once-clear, plastic, super-sized lunch box, with which I was presented. On opening I discovered dinner inside.

And what a dinner it was. In the box were two large pieces of pork, together with pumpkin, sweet potato and boiled greens similar to Warrigal greens. I was initially concerned about the pork being properly cooked but it turned out to be the best pork I can ever recall eating. It was moist and tender with a delightful flavour. Providing an ingestion of protein that my body craved but was not used to, so fearing repercussions I declined the offer of a second helping. Dinner, brought to me so that I was the first to eat, was a display of respect, kindness and thoughtfulness by this community.

Later in Eric's hut about twenty men and women sat around the fire. Most of the first search team were there with all the clan and village leaders as well as the leader of the second search team.

Again the stories were told of the our trip up the mountain. The freezing cold, the new lands and *The Flying Dutchman* search. It turned out that the second search party was rained out. They had followed our trail to the grassland, set up camp and started searching. The rain began at about 1pm and didn't let up, so they left while it still rained the following day.

I presented my findings and future plans to the group. There was much discussion about the new location, and future searches and most importantly the idea of two semi-permanent camps with new trails, which I pointed out on the map. I knew that the trails would not be cut to match any map but would be cut to suit the terrain ... but as close as possible to where I indicated on the map. I explained how the tracks must be made safe for trekkers. It is important to leave no spikes where small trees and shrubs are cut on a sharp angle. Steep sections must have steps or foot holes, or be zig-zagged.

Enthusiasm returned to the group when they knew I intended to run a trek even if we hadn't found *The Flying Dutchman*. To keep the excitement going I offered a 300 Kina reward to the first person to locate the wreck and send me pictures. The amount is two weeks wages for a security guard in Port Moresby but where villagers are largely self sufficient, 300 Kina can supplement a family for a considerable time.

I went to sleep that night thinking more about home, but regretting that I did not have additional days to search. I imagined what the wreck would now look like. In a fleeting, wishful thought, I imagined deferring my flight and returning to the mountains, to search there for another week ...

Passing thoughts ... I was ready for home and had pushed myself physically. Another week in the tropical jungle would be too much. I am looking forward to getting home to Meryl. I feel a little touch of loneliness on my solo adventure.

Chapter 14

DAY ONE OF THE WALKOUT — KINDNESS AND HORROR

True to PNG-style our early departure was late by my standards but I was not worried because we only had to get to Tabu that night. The relaxed start meant plenty of time for breakfast. I devoured the last of the muesli and managed a cup of coffee. I was going to eat a small can of spaghetti but decided to leave that for later. Regaining weight could wait till I got back to home cooking.

There were nine men with me, Wairi, Bardey, Nick, Didibu, Gary, Breibio, Kuname and two others whose names I don't know.

Gary was eleven-years old when I walked with him in 2011, on a trip with my then twenty-three-year-old son Jake, from Port Moresby to Laronu. Now nineteen Gary was doing the return journey carrying a 20 kilogram pack containing mostly raw peanuts to sell in Port Moresby.

It was a sad trip for Kuname who was in his early twenties. He was banished from the village because a relationship he had struck up with a village girl was not condoned by his parents. Tradition demanded that Kuname could not return until a husband was found for the girl and she had left to live in her husband's village.

Kuname had always lived in Laronu and was the toughest, strongest and most agile man on our trip into the mountains. He was also a great hunter. I was concerned about what he would do in Port Moresby. If he didn't find somewhere to apply his talents he could easily become a fearsome *rascal* — the term used for a criminal in PNG.

Unemployment is very high in PNG. Many young people leave their villages looking for jobs or a better life and end up in the main towns – Port Moresby, Popondetta, Lae being the main ones. To survive they turn to crime, often fueled by alcohol. They roam in gangs and as individuals. They are referred to a Rascals. Those towns are only safe if you make sure you respect the need for security and do not put yourself at risk by venturing into the wrong area or at the wrong time. It would be too easy for Kuname to join one of those gangs.

Nick and I led the way to Tabu with Wairi close behind, whilst the others finished packing and saying goodbye to families. Seven of them would not be returning in the near future.

The walk back along the Mimai River from Laronu to Igonomu took less than three hours. A magnificent walk beside the river. This river which ends up becoming the Kemp Welsh River flows south to the coast. In the mountains the Mimai is cold, rushing over rapids and beautifully blue and clear. This was my first walk in the southerly direction along the river and I admired the scenery of jungle interspersed with small villages as I processed the events of the trip.

Replanning the June trek occupied my mind. And how to develop business and income once I got home. I needed more income to be able to afford to do the things I love and to help these communities. These reflections and recalling

Day one of the walkout — kindness and horror

this incredible journey, cemented my intention to record my experiences for my own benefit and to tell the story to others. I wrote when we stopped overnight at Tabu.

Along the Mimai there was time to video the river and the trail. How did I not video more on other parts of the trip? A small Sony camera was reasonably convenient but it was impossible to use in rain. Or when both hands were needed as well as feet to keep me on the trail. I thought, a GoPro or similar would be more suitable to conditions and capture everything that happens. But so much footage would take a lot of time to edit ... perhaps next time.

Nick, Wairi and I reached Igonomu at 11.30am and we rested for about twenty minutes expecting the others to catch up. We passed the time speaking with an elder and his wife who were curious about our journey. Nick and Wairi did most of the talking and the *Igonomuians* were fascinated by the tale. On past trips I had been impressed by the friendliness and hospitality shown to me by the villagers in Igonomu. During our short rest I had the feeling of being *at home* there.

Keen to get to Tabu before the rain started, we pushed on. The trail was mostly uphill from here, with one big steep drop to a river then a long climb up into Tabu. The next village to go through was Sari— where I had attended to Koko's hand just nine days ago. I was both curious and concerned as to what had happened to her slashed hand.

Despite having walked for three hours and it being the hottest part of the day, the short rest at Igonomu had refreshed me and I led the way up the first climb. On approaching Sari we regrouped as it can be a shock to villagers if a white person wanders through their village without being accompanied by local people.

How was Koko? One of three things could have happened. The wounds were clean, Koko was okay and was home in the village. Or she was there but the wound was infected, needing cleaning, perhaps antibiotics and re-dressing. Or that the infection had advanced and she had taken the advice to go to Port Moresby, or at least Kwikila, for medical attention, and her small finger stitched perhaps.

I asked Nick, would he enquire about Koko. The initial response was that she was not here. I was relieved, she has gone, perhaps to Port Moresby? Thank goodness she left to get medical attention. But the story changed. Yes, she has gone. Gone back to her husband in a village even further away from medical assistance. I hope this meant her wounds were healing but I knew that her little finger would be was too damaged. If by some chance infection had not taken hold she would forever have a partially unusable finger. PNG ... this country. I feel exasperated but force myself to accept the way the people deal with injury and tragedy. My consolation is that at least I have an opportunity to make a small difference.

For our kindness Koko's family gave us a large cucumber each and armed with this belated lunch we set off. As we departed the village I mused on a world bartering economy where medical attention is paid with vegetables. Or maybe when they are undervalued they get peanuts?

We finished the first climb and bathed in sweat after the exertion in near forty degrees, at the highest point we sat down in the shade to enjoy the cucumbers. Nick extracted a pineapple from his pack and skillfully cutting off the skin with his machete, he handed me half of the juicy flesh. To balance out the fruit and vegetables I tried chewing a few hard tack biscuits but dry food was difficult to swallow. That weight gain program will start when I get home.

By early afternoon we had dropped altitude, crossed the river and were a third of the way up the circa 400 metre climb into Tabu. Well before coming to the first huts we came across a large group of people resting on the side of the trail next to a large abundant vegetable garden. The group was devouring several watermelons and pineapples. Did they just help themselves to the produce from the garden? Only if one of them belonged to the family who owned the garden.

It turned out the group was led by Gilbert, the school teacher for Dorobisoro. Gilbert and his wife who was also a school teacher, were returning from Port Moresby to open the school for the year. I noted that it was already a week after school had officially started. Perhaps the first week is taken up with travelling time? Gilbert told me that this year they were starting a year eight class for the first time, which was good news. Until then, year eight students would most likely travel to Kwikila or Port Moresby and stay with *Won Tok, (relatives)*.

What books does the school need? I asked. They need the year eight curriculum texts because they have none………..Yep…..PNG. I told him we would get some of those year eight books to him if I was able to come back on the planned June trip.

The water melons and pineapples had been picked and placed at the side of the trail by Siage Lori, Nick's father and Bardey's father-in-law, from Tabu. Siage had heard we were coming and had gone to his garden specially to pick the fruit and vegetables for us. He was waiting there when the school group had come through so he offered the produce to them, for which they were grateful.

When we turned up he and Nick disappeared into the garden for more watermelons. We feasted on melons till we could eat no more. This gesture of Siage's represents the kindness and thoughtfulness of many of these remote village people. Watermelon juice was our power source for the very hot climb up into Tabu.

Siage's kindness reminded me later that afternoon that a few years ago when I was visiting Tabu with a group of trekkers, Siage had a badly cut and infected hand. I tended to the wound, cleaning it and using antibiotic cream as the others ate lunch. Kindness repays kindness, and was that more vegetables for medical assistance?.

We arrived, hot and sweaty in Tabu before the rain. It turned out we were well in front of the rest of the group, who came into the village hours later. I changed into some dryish clothes and crashed for an hour of sleep. The rest of the party and my food arrived at 6.30pm and by then I was hanging out for a cup of soup to replace the salt I had lost during the day.

Whilst waiting for everyone to arrive I had time to myself to recall the second day of my journey into these lands. The day I was planning to cancel the trip and catch a helicopter out of Laronu because I had no communications home and was absolutely knackered by the trek. The ups-and-downs of the trip had been as much physical as emotional.

I felt quite at home in the open guest house belonging to Siage. I squatted, as best I could, by the fire and tried to make something of the chatter amongst Wairi, Siage, Didibu and Nick. How uncomfortable this is likely to be to outside people who aren't used to such basic living conditions. The rain blew in. The smoke from the fire was sometimes choking. And wet clothes never dry. Why did I feel so at home? I think that it has a lot to do with feeling secure and trusting the people with whom I travelled, also the kindness shown to me, the beauty and simplicity of life, and probably knowing that I would not be living like this forever.

I knew I would miss all of this. Sometime in the near future I will retire from what some might consider an extreme sport. Being a trek leader on Kokoda was *a walk in the park* compared to trails I had recently trekked, let alone the challenge of leading groups of people over the Ghost Mountain or *Kapa Kapa* Trails.

The experiences of the previous few days replayed in my conscious thoughts. We went up on Ghost Mountain and beyond. We had been to places that local people had never

Day one of the walkout — kindness and horror

been, even though it was their own land. I recalled how the men and dogs hunted possum, cus cus and tree kangaroo. How they with the dogs help had found bush turkey nests and gathered bush turkey eggs. All at 3,080 metres above sea level. Memories returned of torrential rain, no clear view of the sky for days, brilliant sunrises and sunsets, and the sights, sounds and smells of village life. These had become normalised and I had failed to appreciate how special it was to experience this way of life, just once. I have trekked the jungle trails so many times that I feel at home here. Right at that moment I was dry, fed and looked after. Or I may have had different thoughts.

I am sad to leave all this behind but happy to be returning to Meryl and our home in Mapleton.

I thought about my legacy to the Trail and all the communities along the way. Several of my travelling companions had asked me who would take over when I stopped making these trips. Would my son take over from me? An automatic question because in this cultural tradition, land and assets are passed from father to first born son.

Would my eldest son be interested? I wondered. I needed to give him the chance to consider it. If he accepted the challenge, this would give me more incentive to continue a while longer. Until he could learn the ropes, and be in a position financially, to take over. I will speak to him and invite him to come on the June trips.

Physically I was feeling strong and could have gone on beyond Tabu that day but I was aware of conserving strength and avoiding the over-exertion that was my downfall on the trip in. My salt intake was also a concern. I did not have enough salt during the day to replace what I sweated out and was down to my last few spoons of Staminade electrolyte replacement.

At about 8pm as I was settling down to sleep, all thoughts disappeared in the light of something serious, which has had a lasting impact on me. Nick asked me to attend to a girl in Tabu, who had *a sore foot.* He had been at the girl's hut and used his phone to take a photo of the foot to show me.

I looked at the photo ... once and then twice more. What was I seeing? What could I do?

It was raining a little and the sticky clay was treacherous to walk on. The girl lived at the top end of the village, at least 400 metres uphill. There was no hesitation. I gathered the first aid kits and went with Nick and Bardey by the light of a head-torch. Along the way we gathered a party of interested bystanders. There were so many standing around the shelter where the girl was seated on small roughhewn stool that I asked Nick and Bardey, to get them to move out of the way.

The girl went to remove the rag wrapped around her toe but I stopped her. From the photo I knew what was underneath. I needed more information before looking at the wound.

The girl's name was Rachel. She was twenty years old and lived with her parents. The problem had started about two to three months earlier with no specific injury. Since then she had been washing her foot in a stream a couple of times a day. I suspected this was done to cool the foot and to relieve pain. Her mother had been bathing the foot once a day in warm water. According to her parents, Rachel cried all night long and did not sleep much.

When I met her she was chewing on fire-roasted corn and did not appear to have a problem with eating.

Rachel described the pain, going right up her leg, and her leg was swelling. From time to time she was taking Amoxycillin — one tablet a day given by someone else who had been prescribed the medicine.

I was prepared when I took off the rag. Others were not prepared. There was a loud gasp as people saw the wound in bright torchlight. In retrospect we should have been without an audience but that is difficult in a village.

Rachel's big toe was swollen to almost the thickness of her wrist. There was an open wound with rotting flesh, dead and exposed bone and a mass of skinless flesh. The wound smelled foul and was weeping greenish fluid.

I cleaned the wound with warm saline water and showing her mother how to do this. I gave instructions and material for ongoing care and a short course of antibiotics that I hoped would be effective in controlling the infection. I also gave her some tablets for pain relief. Rachel's pain must have been ten-out-of-ten and constant, yet when I cleaned the wound she did not complain.

Rachel needed more help than a traveller's first aid kit could provide. She needed surgery and the toe probably required amputation to save the leg ... and possibly her life. She must get to Port Moresby urgently, I stressed.

Less than a day's walk from Tabu is Dorobisoro the nearest first aid post. Rachel had not been taken there, but it would not have made a difference. The para-medical officer had still not returned from his walk to Port Moresby, a three to four day journey to get the medical supplies he had been without for some time. He would also be challenged to get the supplies back to the village as this would require a government-funded charter flight.

You can imagine my thoughts when much later than usual, I tried to sleep that night.

I have been told by many sources that pre independence a regular medical service and medicine was available to even the remotest of villages. The government patrol officer called *Kiaps* would make sure that injured people were attended to, arranging transport for them if they needed to get to a hospital. It saddened me to know that the breakdown of this system had resulted in countless lives lost.

Chapter 15

MY CONVICTION IS REINFORCED

I did not sleep well and was up early. It was a pleasure to get ready for the day ahead.

I had woken many times with images of Rachel's toe haunting me. She would need skin grafts as a minimum but was unlikely to get that treatment in Port Moresby General Hospital. Her parents did not have money to take her elsewhere. More likely her toe would be amputated followed by a long healing process. The loss of a big toe would make it difficult to walk on the uneven terrain but there was probably no choice.

Would the antibiotics be enough to control the infection? On previous trips I had been surprised by the difference just a little antibiotic made.

I recalled a lady called Pamela in another remote village about fifty kilometres to the north-east of Tabu. A friend and I gave her first aid treatment for what looked like an almost untreatable tropical ulcer consuming her leg. The bone was exposed and she had lost half her body weight. We had organised a helicopter but she refused to go so we gave her a week's worth of antibiotics, electrolytes to help with rehydration, pain relief tablets and care instructions.

We did not know what happened to Pamela for two years. Until back on another trek and we apprehensively returned to the village. Pamela was not to be seen anywhere. We worked up the courage to ask after her. Oh yes Pamela. She is out in the garden. You could not imagine how relieved we were and almost in disbelief that she had survived. Pamela was one tough and persistent woman.

I hoped Rachel would be the same. But I knew that even if the antibiotics did their job, she still needed surgery and something done with the dead bone protruding from the wound.

Didibu was organising a flight from Port Moresby to Dorobisoro in a fortnight, in relation to a funeral. I gave Didibu 300 Kina to get Rachel on the flight to Port Moresby. She really needed immediate medical attention, but I figured, she had survived two months, another two weeks with antibiotics will be a breeze.

I packed and had breakfast. The usual six Weetbix with powdered milk, topped off with fresh pineapple slices and a cup of coffee.

Then I waited for the *early start* ... today at 8.30am. It was difficult for my companions to leave, given the hospitality and food they were receiving. Bowls of cooked vegetables corn, yam, pumpkin and greens kept appearing ... and they just kept eating.

Whilst their meal was in progress I thought about the people I had treated for ailments on this trip which was about ten, excluding really minor cuts. The first aid kit was depleted but I had made it without needing antibiotics myself. Just as well because I had dispensed nearly all of my first aid supplies, not a large quantity to begin with.

Our destination for that day was Lora. The village to which we had arrived in the rain just ten days ago on the journey in the opposite direction. The plan was to overnight there, leave before light tomorrow, get to the road-head and pick up a PMV to be in Port Moresby by tomorrow night.

As you might have guessed by now, being PNG, a plan is just a plan. You always need a plan B and often a plan C. That day was no different ...

I left Tabu with a heavy heart for Rachel. On checking how she was in the morning I was told she had the best sleep for weeks and was feeling good. That was probably the effect of the paracetamol. I knew severe pain would return if the infection continued. There was little more I could do, apart from chartering a flight, hiring a surgeon and an operating theatre in a private hospital in Port Moresby. I had to move on emotionally and physically.

For the first three hours we travelled fairly fast and I felt strong. Only two steep down-and-ups before resting for lunch at the village of Otah. Here I hit a real flat spot — to do mainly with my lack of sleep and state of mind. The fact that I had walked hard for four hours in hot, energy-sapping conditions, on a breakfast of six Weetbix also had something to do with it. After eating a few dry biscuits, peanut butter by the spoonful, slices of salami and pineapple, and having a rest, I was ready for the next up-down-up to Lora.

Alas at Otah we were told of three women with flu-like symptoms who had been sick for a week or two. I feel helpless when it comes to treating this type of condition. There is nothing to treat influenza, if in fact that was what it was. I had no ability to diagnose diseases and illnesses apart from my life experience and wilderness first aid training.

I questioned for symptoms from a distance, without exposing myself to the patients who had aches and pains, coughs and sneezing, and possible fever but that was hard to ascertain. I gave them some of the last stocks of paracetamol and suggested they eat more pineapple, of which they had many, in the hope these provided enough Vitamin C to help.

For my trouble I was given two large cucumbers and a small bag of raw peanuts. Only the previous day at Sari I had been musing about *medical assistants* being paid peanuts.

We arrived in Lora about 3.30pm. It was sunny and hot the temperature above thirty-five degrees C. I relaxed by stretching out on the rough wooden deck under a hut for a short time. Nick informed me after that our host, the village elder, had been worried about me when we last stayed in Lora.

He had thought I should not have to walk down the hill to the *long-drop* fifty metres behind the hut. Whist we were away he had gone to the trouble to build a toilet just for me that was closer, just ten metres from the hut. He had dug another pit and had built a roof and walls. I suspect he solicitored some others to help in this display of incredible kindness and thoughtfulness. The builder was thrilled when I said in local dialect, it is *myna myna, very good*.

As I started to settle into my accommodation for a much sought after rest, I was asked to attend a woman in the village, *who is sick*. All day I had been in anguish over Rachel. And then there were the three women at Otah. Now I was confronted by Ugaru a fifty-something year old woman with a massive tropical ulcer on her thigh. The stench of rotting flesh was unmistakable. Ugaru's skin had a very large big black patch that looked like her leg had been charred. There was a foul, thick green discharge from the ulcerated area.

Yes, she reported, she had been cleaning it ... scrubbing with Omo washing powder once a day and with salt water twice a day. It had been more swollen and is now, less swollen.

I had given away the last of my skin-infection-specific antibiotics to Rachel and there were no rubber gloves left so I did not touch the wound.

Ugaru, I said, stop the Omo. Salt water, yes. You must bathe these wounds five times a day in salt water. Put in a spoon full of salt into that container of boiled water. Wash and boil the rags. Use clean boiled rags each time. Wash your hands before washing the wounds. I will try to get antibiotics in Port Moresby to send to you.

Later, I searched right through everything in my pack for any remaining medical supplies and found a two-day dose of an antibiotic that just might work. I gave these to Ugaru knowing that a longer dose was needed.

Wherever possible I avoid the use of antibiotics because of the impact it has in reducing natural resistance to infection. I definitely did not want to make these people antibiotic dependent. After all they had for many years used naturally available plants for medicine. Some of that knowledge has been lost. In the case of Rachel and Ugaru I felt their chances of survival were limited and they needed all the help they could get.

Every time I see a PNG national with tropical ulcers I recall the stories from Australians imprisoned by the Japanese in World War Two, to work on the Burma rail line. They had little if any medication, and antibiotics in the form of Penicillin, was as yet not available. The doctors there had a lot of success boiling rags and applying them frequently to the soldiers tropical ulcers. I am drawing on that experience here, and hoping it will be effective.

That night I talked to Meryl at length… regardless of generating a large satellite phone bill. I was distraught at my inability to provide the degree of care needed by Koko, Rachel, the three women in Otah and Ugaru.

These experiences have re-enforced the purpose for the trip to find *The Flying Dutchman*. The only long term solution for the people in the communities is to improve PNG government-provided medical and education services.

I wasn't looking for it but I got the strongest message on that journey from Laronu to Port Moresby. The message seemed to resonate in my head, what I am doing is absolutely what is needed. I feel destined to be here. Those I had met, who were ill and needed help, were shocking reminders for me to keep doing what I can to bring better services to the people living in village communities. Up to that time I hadn't believed in a calling. But if I did that was it. Now I have a sense of what that means.

This gave me renewed conviction to see that *The Flying Dutchman* venture is successful. Getting people involved to raise awareness and show by example how practical help can be provided, is the most effective action. Let Koko, Rachel, Ugaru circumstances be examples that will bring attention to the plight of the communities in this part of PNG.

I carried this conviction to my meal that night and ate as much as possible of the rice, noodles, bully beef and spaghetti sauce. Not a big meal but the best I could do on a stomach that had considerably shrunk over the last twelve days. I needed as much sustenance as I could for the ten-hour-plus walk starting at 5am. I wasn't looking forward to the walk but it was the last day so I would dig deep, knowing I could recover once I got to Port Moresby.

At least that was what I thought. As usual what actually happened is another matter altogether.

Chapter 16

UNLUCKY FOR SOME AND JUST PLAIN HARD WORK FOR OTHERS

Breakfast at 4am was the usual six Weetbix, plus a handful of peanuts. How the heck will I get through this day? I pondered. The longest day of the whole trip. I needed more sustenance and my plan was to get through on a sugar fix. I was prepared. I had with me some ghastly Chinese-made lollies, all that I could find in Port Moresby on my arrival two weeks ago. Guaranteed to have plenty of glucose. I was relying on this to provide energy throughout the day because it was going to be a long day. Little did I know how long.

Before leaving Lora I looked forward to trying out the new *long-drop* that had been built for me. By head-torchlight I headed off along the short path to the new outhouse for my morning ritual. To say the experience was most uncomfortable is an understatement.

The first difficulty was that my host and the builder had underestimated my height. In order to get inside the door of the new *dunny*, I was forced to drop my pants and assume a shallow squat, before going through the doorway. Bending from the waist, eyes to the ground I shuffled and backed into position. A position made even more awkward and precarious because the opening over the hole was small and unstable around the edges. What this has taught me is to stand taller when I am with architects and builders. It is the thought that counts. All the same I was glad I would probably use this toilet only once in my life.

We started with a good omen. For the first time during the whole trip we started nearly at the planned time and by 5.30am we were heading off with head-torches on. Twenty minutes into the walk we could just see the track without torches. We moved quickly and after thirty minutes I was sweating freely in the ninety percent humidity. I was not alone, Nick and the others were also feeling the heat.

Bardey's plan was to call the PMV driver from a vantage point where there was supposed to be mobile phone coverage. I cringed recalling similar plans on more than one occasion during the inwards journey. Bardey would arrange for the driver to be waiting at the road-head, regardless of what time we arrived there.

One of my stress reduction techniques for PNG is to not believe any plan until it actually happens. And to have a backup plan. Today I was in Bardey's hands. He knows the local schedules, and is familiar with the trail and the people. Fortunately, *don't believe it till it happens* saved my sanity that day.

The climb to the mobile phone reception point took four-and-a-half hours of solid fast walking. Fast for me but probably just a good pace for my companions. Good progress, I thought. We are pretty much on time.

However, it was not too long before Plan A unwound. First, Bardey's phone was not working. He borrowed another. Then tried mine. But no number of phones or combinations of phones and SIM cards enabled him to raise the PMV driver.

Looks like Plan B, I thought. That is, get to the road-head and hope to catch the last PMV of the day.

Hard walking in high humidity and forty degree heat saps energy and while Bardey tried the various phone options, I dozed for a short while under a tree. Then he and the others also took a nap. Apparently it wasn't just me who felt drained.

If the walk was to be ten hours all up, that meant another five-and-a-half hours tough walking. Recalling that first downhill scramble in the dusk on the way in, the last leg was a steep climb of 300 to 400 metres elevation on an incline fully exposed to the sun.

I needed more food so I consumed one-eighth of a pineapple, a whole large cucumber and a handful of raw peanuts. Not much to fuel the physical exertion of the day, but literally as much as I could stomach. I estimated my weight loss on the trip must be six to seven kilograms, and my fat reserves were negligible.

I mixed up the last spoonful of Staminaide. As I shook the water bottle, I promised myself, to keep it for the very last push up the steep climb to the road-head. Whenever that might be.

We spent nearly an hour-and-a-half at that spot, with Bardey periodically attempting to contact the PMV driver. Eventually I suggested we get on with Plan B. Let's just walk out now.

Thirty minutes from the rest spot we went through a gap on a high ridge from where Nick pointed out our destination. The junction was on the road-head up on a ridge-line, way to the south. A roof of a hut on the destination ridge-line glinted. That's all I could see. The junction road-head was so far away that nothing else was visible. It was a spec on the horizon.

We would eventually come out there but right then it looked like a full day's walk. We had walked half a day and between us and the road-head were three ridges and three rivers. I doubted we were able to cover the terrain in time to catch a PMV in daylight hours. I was not confident that my body could handle the three up-and-downs over that distance.

At the next river crossing I felt over-hot and following my companions dropped into the water fully clothed. Immersed in the cool, clear but shallow water, my overheated core temperature dropped to a reasonable level.

After that I was well enough to eat some crumbling hard tack biscuits with peanut butter gouged out of the plastic container. I ate as much as I could, hoping the food would eventually translate to energy in the parts of the body where it was needed. I also ate the last remaining and treasured muesli bar, cranberry and chocolate.

After another up-and-down and another rocky river crossing we struggled up a sun exposed ridge to the village of Odika. Everybody was bathed in sweat, running down our arms and heads, and dripping off noses. The climb in extreme heat, extracted tremendous energy and determination. On reaching a patch of shade at the edge of the village, we all dropped to the ground.

There were plans in Odika for a funeral the next day. We were asked, or perhaps it was volunteered as is the custom, for donations to the funeral. My companions offered the usual currency of betel nut and I gave a few Kina. Trading with the women of the village followed ... betel nut exchanged for ripe bananas.

Whilst my companions frequently chewed betel nut which gave them spurts of energy I had to resort to other means.

It was at Odika that I received something which enabled me to complete the walk, and to continue with renewed energy. Sam is one of the family heads in Odika, who had joined our party nearly two weeks ago on the way in, intending to go to Ghost Mountain. However, after reaching and staying at Laronu for a day, he had been recalled to his village, partially due to the funeral preparations. I had given Sam a few Kina in Laronu before his return. Now he came up with *gold* for our group — ten large, fresh and full coconuts.

Using a sharpened bamboo stake Sam dehusked the coconuts. Bush knives came out to cut a piece from the hard shell and soon we were all drinking coconut water. I felt an immediate and amazing revitalising effect. Previous experience and stories had informed me that coconut water is an excellent source of electrolytes, including SSGT Holleman's survival account when his group trekked from *The Flying Dutchman* crash site.

With renewed energy I led the group up the next steep, exposed incline and down the other side to the river. I felt strong going up that hill, however at one stage my heart, with a pounding that resonated in my ears, reminded me to back off.

After another 100 metre elevation climb we plunged downhill to the last river crossing before the final climb to the junction. The water seemed less cool than at the last river, but when I stretched out in it, my elevated core temperature again dropped significantly.

I felt fresh for about fifteen minutes. During that last severely steep and exposed climb the temperature, humidity and physical strain kept our pace in check. At the predetermined altitude I drank the last of the Staminade, which helped me to finish the final stretch. Surprisingly I did not collapse on reaching the junction, perhaps because of the two electrolyte replacement drinks. After seeing-in and welcoming all my companions as they emerged at the top of the trail, I lay down with my head in a patch of shade for a fifteen minute rest.

Bardey was the last to make it to the road. He had clearly been over-extended. He struggled sweating and stumbling up to where the rest of the group were waiting. Not only was he physically suffering but he was vague and in some mental confusion. Mild heatstroke, I thought.

Now we waited. Apart from the cries of birdlife in the not too distant jungle, there was no other activity, not a single vehicle nor pedestrians. By 6.30pm, still no sign of a PMV.

I roused Bardey, giving him the satellite phone to call the PMV driver.

The driver answered. Great, I thought. We will have a PMV here soon. But alas no. His vehicle was out of commission ... a differential *bugger-up*.

It was starting to get dark so we invoked Plan C. Walking a couple of kilometres to the closest village. See if we can stay with someone for the night. Catch a PMV in the morning ...

I led the way, consumed in thoughts and hoping it was only two kilometres. I had woken at 4am. Started walking at 5.30am. And walked till 6.00pm. With about two and a half hours rest over the day, what had I eaten? I made a mental list. Six Weetbix, two handfuls of raw peanuts, one-eighth of a pineapple, a large cucumber, a muesli bar, a banana, coconut water, a dry biscuit or two, a couple of scoops of peanut butter, a teaspoon of Staminade and ten horrible lollies. What had my body endured? Walking up-and-down five ridges, humidity over ninety percent and temperature above thirty-five degrees Centigrade. I should be so lucky. Another two kilometres? No problem ...

We arrived at the outskirts of a village. In the dark I could make out a few men wandering around with machetes. They did not seem to be in any hurry. Were they dangerous and walking with purpose? I felt safe being with the group of men I knew.

Didibu disappeared into the darkness and returned in just a few minutes with another PMV operator who kindly agreed to allow us to stay at his place overnight. I was relieved. Really looking forward to somewhere to rest. To getting a decent feed. Perhaps even a wash? Or so I imagined ...

I followed the group to our host's place, which was a five minute walk between a few huts. However once there it was not apparent that we were welcome. The family was quiet without the usual greeting or conversation with our group. Instead everybody sat in silence, waiting for something to happen. I exercised patience knowing something would eventually happen.

After an hour, the PMV driver turned up. A plan was hatched. He would take us to Boregaina, the next main village, in the morning. To catch the early morning PMV to Port Moresby. Really good news, I thought. Hopeful but accepting this may be another plan subject to *the PNG factor*.

Now it was 8.30 or 9.00 o'clock and there was no sign of food, no mention of where to sleep. There we were, a group of ten from Laronu. Everybody was more than tired. Bardey had collapsed and using hot water from our host I was feeding him cups of instant chicken noodle soup and making him drink as much as he could. He needed both water and salts from that soup.

I made some indirect enquiries. Everyone was waiting for us, meaning me, to provide food … the PMV operator, the driver and fifteen or so people who were family, plus a few friends.

Three of us made for the trade store about 300 metres away. Even though it was late, the storekeeper was still in his store, which was also the front part of his hut. We purchased three one kilogram bags of rice, four large bags of noodles, one large can of tuna and two cans of curried chicken.

At our host's place the women of the household were soon boiling all the rice in a huge black pot on the fire, in the middle of the grassy area outside the house. It wasn't long before the first enormous serve of white rice with curried chicken was brought to me heaped on a large flat tin plate, by one of the women. I reluctantly sampled the curried chicken. And promptly added a small can of baked beans, the last of my travelling store, because the canned chicken with bones, did not appeal to my palate, despite my hunger.

The food we provided fed our crew, the host and a few of his friends, and about twenty of their family members. Fair payment for our group to camp outside their house for the night. At 10.30 or 11pm I was shown to a room in one of the houses where I was to sleep.

I rolled out the sleeping bag and collapsed on top of it without bothering about the mosquitoes. The PMV operator and driver were in loud conversation as I fell asleep. The chances of departing on time were pretty slim but I would get up at 4am, just in case the 4.30 departure actually happened.

Until then I slept ... too tired to remember any dreams.

Chapter 17

A NOT-SO-SIMPLE TRIP TO PORT MORESBY

My last day on the trail, before returning to the metropolis of Port Moresby.

That morning surprised me again. Everybody woke at 4am and we left right on 4.30. I was ecstatic. Perhaps we will run moderately to time today? I planned an early arrival at the hotel and what I would do today.

The vehicle we started out on before sunrise was not licensed to carry passengers. So the driver stuck to the backroad and did a hand-over at Boregaina. The PMV operators there don't like going up to the junction in any case because they consider the roads to be dangerous, difficult and slow to traverse.

Those Boregainian operators had it right. The rough track ran along a ridge beside drop-offs and through washouts that would raise hairs on the back of a seasoned four-wheel driver. We bounced along in the dark. Our previous night's host rode on the back *spruiking* the trip to Boregaina and Kwikila to any of the huts and villages along the way. The driver used the horn liberally announcing the available ride.

No one living along that road would sleep-in that morning. The truck stopped in a number of places, to pick up people.

Outside a small village of no more than four huts, the PMV hit a pedestrian. There was bang at the side of the vehicle. Followed by shouts. The driver stopped, then backed up to see what had happened. An inebriated middle aged male was calmly sitting in the grass at the side of the road, apparently unaffected by the ordeal, so the driver went on.

Covered in dust, we arrived in Boregaina around 6am. We entered the yard of a reasonable house where our PMV was waiting. Or so we thought, until it started and was driven right past us into the village. So much for a quick transfer and off to Port Moresby, I thought. The only thing to do was to wait patiently for the next revelation. And to work out today's Plan B.

That truck took an hour going around the streets of Boregaina before returning loaded with produce for market in Port Moresby. Great cane baskets and woven string *billums,* recycled PVC rice bags containing mostly green bananas, were packed tightly under the wooden plank seats and all the way up the centre of the truck tray.

By that time there were about thirty people waiting. I looked at the load then at the passengers. It would be a bit crowded for the three or four hour drive to Port Moresby.

I was wrong ... it would be more than a *bit crowded.* Another ten or so clambered on board for the trip to the first stop of Kwikila. Just before that village the driver stopped to pick up half a dozen school children. Crowded wasn't the word. More like jam-packed.

As we entered Kwikila I recalled the Police Station two weeks prior and deliberately kept a low profile. A bit difficult to hide amongst a truck load of PNG nationals. But perhaps I had tanned after two weeks in the jungle, because fortunately I was not hauled off to the Police Station. I would have liked to call in to there for closure to my previous experience but didn't ask because it would result in further delay.

Bardey, said, as soon as we get to Port Moresby, we will go to the hotel to drop you off first. That will be nice, I thought. I might even be at the hotel by mid morning.

But others had more influence on the priorities. First, because it was more convenient, Wairi, Didibu and the other Laronu men were dropped off. The driver took half an hour and three circuits of the streets before finding the right one. Because of the lack of street numbers and street signs, it is difficult finding any address in Port Moresby – even if there was a street directory.

I said goodbye to the crew, apart from Bardey and Nick, who wanted to travel with me to the hotel. I was sad leaving everyone, unsure when I would see them again but hoping it would be just four months in the future.

Priority for the driver was to deliver the produce to the Port Moresby wholesale fresh food market. He was really a trader who had bought the produce in Boregaina and was supplying it to sellers at the market. Money from us for the trip had been a bonus for him.

The wholesale market could only be described as semi-organised chaos. Ten or more PMVs were backed into a narrow space over the kerb outside one of the gates so that people and produce could offload into the market area. The produce was manhandled all the way, mostly on the heads of men. Our PMV was unloaded slowly, one produce-load and one payment at a time, until after two hours, well after midday, all the produce was gone. Only empty baskets and bags were stacked for return to their owners in Boregaina.

As the last passenger I was taken to my hotel, accompanied only by Nick because Bardey left thirty minutes earlier, tired of waiting and keen to get home to his wife. Nick and I walked the 200 metres together from where the PMV dropped us at the side of the road to the hotel entrance.

As we entered the air conditioned foyer I was deeply moved by both a sense of relief and of great sadness. Relief because I was really on my way home and probably more in control of my destiny than I had been for two weeks. Sadness because I was leaving a world of daily surprises and new experiences. I was leaving the rawness of the remote country. And I was leaving people and companions who gave me incredible experiences, which many others from my world would never have. Nor perhaps even believe.

Epliogue

When I started the journey to find *The Flying Dutchman* I had an idea what would happen. The local people knew where the plane was. I also had a reasonable knowledge from the research. I would trek to the location. The locals would show me the wreck and I would verify it, planning the logistics for a fundraising trek as I went.

Well, it certainly didn't pan out like that.

The surprise elements of PNG and my personal challenges had changed the agenda every day of the trip, without fail. It was a roller coaster journey both physically and emotionally.

You might say it was a total failure because we did not find *The Flying Dutchman*.

On another level it was incredibly successful.

Maybe I am a *Flying Dutchman* of a sort, because I found out a lot about myself on this unique adventure. I ended the trip with a renewed conviction that the intention to help the communities along The Ghost Mountain Trail is absolutely the right thing to do.

Many months after returning from that journey I found out via many words-of-mouth, that at least two of those I had helped with injuries, Rachel from Tabu and Ugaru from Lora both survived. Rachel is back at school but reportedly limping somewhat, and Ugaru is back to "normal" being a hard working member of the community. It brings tears to my eyes even now to know that they are now well, at least until the next injury…

As 2020 was the year of COVID19 my plans to return with a fundraising trek did not eventuate.

Acknowledgements

There are so many people to whom I am grateful — for allowing and supporting me to take on the adventure, and for helping me to keep safe along the way.

First and foremost Meryl, my wife for her crazy belief in me and trust that I could get myself there and back safely. And for being the operations manager at the end of the Satellite Phone – once we got it working. Meryl has shared the highs and lows, of an on-again-off-again trip.

John Brady (ex-*Kiap*) and members of the Mapleton Men's Shed. Without being asked they donated money for warm sleeping bags and clothing for my travelling companions in PNG. This was vital on the summit of Ghost Mountain.

James Campbell, author of *Ghost Mountain Boys*, for his ongoing support and collaboration in our joint venture to helping people along the Ghost Mountain Trail.

All my travelling companions in PNG, especially Bardey, Wairi, and Didibu whose support for me, for their communities and for the cause, made the trip possible and successful. All of them gave up their time and made other personal sacrifices to support the initiative, knowing in the long run it will give hope to their home villages so desperately in need of basic services.

And to Nick for giving special attention to me during the entire trip, helping me whenever it looked like I needed a hand.

Thanks also to those who have contributed to the editing – keeping the story true but making it far more interesting to read: Rosemary Gemmel, Lenore Tonks, many thanks.

Bruce Hoy, ex curator of the PNG Museum for allowing me to use the photograph of the Flying Dutchman on the cover of this book. Bruce is likely to be the last person other than locals to visit the crash site, which he did in 1986.

The Ghost Mountain or Kapa Kapa Trail taken by US troops in 1942.

The track taken to reach the Flying Dutchman search area.

The track from Laronu to the search area up over Ghost Mountain.

My youngest travelling companion on the trek in to Laronu.

The Ghost Mountain guest house run by Eric at Laronu.

The author on the trail above Laronu heading towards Ghost Mountain.

The search team rests prior to tackling Ghost Mountain.

Didibu (front) and Wairi (rear) showing the route to the search area.

The author and camp on Ghost Mountain.

Kumani (left) and Nick (right) sporting donated shirts on Ghost Mountain.

Views from the summit of Ghost Mountain.

Camp Hope – the closest camp to the Flying Dutchman search area.

Grasslands on the southern side of Ghost Mountain.

Saigi surprises us with watermelon prior to our climb into Tabu. (Right to left Wairi, Saigi, Saigi's grandson, and Nick (Saigi's son)).

Stopping for a swim to cool down.

(Wairi & author).

At the roadhead on our trek out. The photo is taken looking back on the country we had walked through that day.

Wairi resting and waiting for the PMV that never came at the roadhead.

www.ingramcontent.com/pod-product-compliance
Lightning Source LLC
Chambersburg PA
CBHW062022290426
44108CB00024B/2747